BEGINNING IN JESUS

6 SMALL GROUP
SESSIONS ON THE
LIFE OF CHRIST

STUDENT EDITION

DOUG FIELDS &
BRETT EASTMAN

ZONDERVAN™

GRAND RAPIDS, MICHIGAN 49530 USA

Youth Specialties

www.youthspecialties.com

Beginning in Jesus, Student Edition: Six Sessions in the life of Christ
Copyright © 2005 by Youth Specialties

Youth Specialties Products, 300 South Pierce Street, El Cajon, CA 92020,
are published by Zondervan, 5300 Patterson Avenue SE, Grand Rapids,
MI 49530

Library of Congress Cataloging-in-Publication Data
Fields, Doug, 1962-
  Beginning in Jesus : six sessions in the life of Christ by / Doug Fields
and Brett Eastman. -- Student ed.
    p. cm.
  ISBN 0-310-26644-0 (pbk.)
  1. Jesus Christ--Person and offices. 2. Christian education--Text-
books for youth.   I. Eastman, Brett, 1959- . II. Title.
BT207.F54 2005
226'.433--dc22

                                    2005015209

Web site addresses listed in this book were current at the time
of publication. Please contact Youth Specialties via e-mail
(YS@YouthSpecialties.com) to report URLs that are no longer
operational and replacement URLs if available.

*Creative Team: Dave Urbanski, Holly Sharp, Mark Novelli, Joanne Heim,
Janie Wilkerson*
Cover Design: Mattson Creative
Printed in the United States of America

05 06 07 08 09 10 / DCI / 10 9 8 7 6 5 4 3 2

ACKNOWLEDGMENTS

This series of six books couldn't have happened if there weren't some wonderful friends who chimed in on the process and added their heart and level of expertise to these pages. I need to acknowledge and thank my friends for loving God, caring for students and supporting me-especially true on this task were Amanda Maguire, Nancy Varner, Ryanne Dearden, Jana Sarti, Matt McGill and the crew at Simply Youth Ministry. I sure appreciate doing life together. Also, I'm very appreciative of Brett Eastman for asking me to do this project.

TABLE OF CONTENTS

INTRODUCTION: READ ME FIRST!

Welcome to a Journey with Jesus (and Others)!

I hope you're ready for God to do something great in your life as you use this book and connect with a few friends and a loving small group leader. The potential of this combination is incredible. The reason we know its potential is because we've heard from thousands of students who've already gone through our first series of LIFETOGETHER books and shared their stories. We've been blessed to hear that the combination of friends gathering together, books with great questions, and the Bible as a foundation have provided the ingredients for life change. As you read these words, know that you're beginning a journey that may revolutionize your life.

The following six sessions are designed to help you grow in your knowledge of Jesus and his teachings and become his devoted disciple. But growth doesn't happen alone. You need God's help and a community of people who love God, too. We've found that a great way to grow strong in Christ is in the context of a caring, spiritual community (or small group). This community is committed to doing life together—at least for a season—and will thrive when each small group member (you) focuses on Jesus as well as the others in the group.

This type of spiritual community isn't easy. It requires several things from you:

- trust
- confidentiality
- honesty
- care
- openness
- risk
- commitment to meet regularly

Anyone can meet with a few people and call it a "group," but it takes stronger commitment and desire to create a spiritual community where others can know you, love you, care for you, and give you the freedom to open up about your thoughts, doubts, and struggles—a place where you're safe to be yourself.

We've learned from the small groups that didn't work that spiritual community can't develop without honesty. Now, at first you may be tempted to show up to your small group session and sit, smile, act nicely, and never speak from your heart—but this type of superficial participation prevents true spiritual community. Please fight through this temptation and know that when you reveal who you really are, you'll contribute something unique and powerful to the group that can't occur any other way. Your honest sharing about your heart and soul will challenge other group members to do the same, and they'll likely become as honest as you are.

To help you get to this place of honesty, every session contains questions that are intended to push you to think, talk, and open your heart. They'll challenge you to expose some of your fears, hurts, and habits. Through them, I guarantee you'll experience spiritual growth and relational intimacy, and you'll build lasting, genuine friendships.

All mature Christians will tell you that God used others to impact their lives. God has a way of allowing one life to connect with another to result in richer, deeper, and more vibrant lives for both. As you go through this book (and the five others in this series), you will have the opportunity to impact someone else—and someone else will have the opportunity to impact you. You'll both become deeper, stronger followers of Jesus Christ. So get ready for some life change.

WHO IS JESUS?

Most people have an opinion about Jesus. But many of these opinions are based on what they've heard or come up with on their own—what they'd prefer Jesus to be—as opposed to their own discovery of Jesus through the Bible. People believe Jesus was all kinds of things—a great teacher, a leader of a revolution, a radical with a political agenda, a gentle man with a big vision, a prophet, a spiritual person who emphasized religion. Still others believe he is who he claimed to be—God.

The Jesus of the Bible is far more compelling than most people's opinions about him. This book, *Beginning in Jesus*, allows you to get to know Jesus as his first followers did. They met Jesus as Teacher, a rabbi. They came to know Jesus as Healer, Shepherd, Servant, Savior, and ultimately the One who defeated death—the risen Lord. From his first words, "Follow me," through his ministry, death, and resurrection, he kept drawing people deeper into God's ways.

Jesus asked his disciples to commit their lives to God's way. As you read the Bible, you'll see that God's ways weren't always easy or comfortable for the disciples to follow. But what motivated them to do what he taught was their rich experience of who he was and all he did for them. *Beginning in Jesus* will ground you in that same experience so you'll more fully desire to follow Jesus and commit to his ways—even when it's not easy or comfortable. The Jesus you're about to encounter is waiting for you to meet him, get closer to him, and commit your life to following his ways and teachings.

When you align your life with Jesus, you're in for a wild, adventurous life. It won't be without its difficulties, but it'll be a better life than you ever dreamed possible.

WHAT YOU NEED TO KNOW ABOUT EACH OF THESE SIX SESSIONS

Each session in this study contains more material than you and your group can complete in a typical meeting of an hour or so. The key to making the most of each session is to choose which questions you'll answer and discuss and which ones you'll save for your alone time. We've tried to make it simple, so if you miss something from one meeting, you can pick it up the next time you're together. Let's be more specific.

Each of the six sessions in *Beginning in Jesus* contains five unique sections. These five sections have the same titles in every book and in every session in the LIFETOGETHER series. The sections are (1) fellowship, (2) discipleship, (3) ministry, (4) evangelism, and (5) worship. These represent five biblical purposes that we believe lead to personal spiritual growth, growth in your student ministry, and health for your entire church. The more you think about these five purposes and try to make them part of your life, the stronger you'll be and the more you'll grow spiritually.

While these five biblical purposes make sense individually, they can make a greater impact when they're brought together. Think of it in sports terms: If you play baseball or softball, you might be an outstanding hitter—but you also need to catch, throw, run, and slide. You need more than one skill to impact your team. In the same way, having a handle on one or two of the five biblical purposes is great—but when they're all reflected together in a person's life, that person is much more biblically balanced and healthy.

You'll find that the material in this book (and in the other LIFETOGETHER books) is built around the Bible. There are a lot of blank spaces and journaling pages where you can write down your thoughts about God's Word and God's work in your life as you explore and live out God's biblical purposes.

Each session begins with a short story that helps introduce the theme. If you have time to read it, great—if not, no big deal. Immediately following the story are five key sections. The following is a brief desrciption of each:

♥ FELLOWSHIP: CONNECTING YOUR HEART TO OTHERS'

Goal: To share about your life and listen attentively to others, caring about what they share

You'll begin your session with a few minutes of conversation that will give you all a chance to share from your own lives, get to know each other better, and offer initial thoughts about the session's theme. The icon for this section is a heart because you're opening up your heart so others can connect with you on a deeper level.

DISCIPLESHIP: GROWING TO BE LIKE JESUS

Goal: To explore God's Word, gain biblical knowledge, and make personal applications

This section will take the most time. You'll explore the Bible and gain some knowledge about Jesus. You'll encounter his life and teachings and discuss how God's Word can make a difference in your own life. The icon for this section is a brain because you're opening your mind to learn God's Word and his ways.

You'll find lots of questions in this section—more than you can discuss during your group time. Your leader will choose the questions you have time to discuss or come up with different questions. We encourage you to respond to the skipped questions on your own; during the week, it's a great way to get more Bible study time.

MINISTRY: SERVING OTHERS IN LOVE

Goal: To recognize and take advantage of opportunities to serve others

When you get to this section, you'll have an opportunity to discuss how to express God's love through serving others. The discussion and opportunities are created to tie into the topic. As you grow spiritually, you'll naturally begin to recognize and take opportunities to serve others. As your heart grows, so will your opportunities to serve. Here, the icon is a foot because feet communicate movement and action—serving and meeting the needs of others requires you to act on what you've learned.

☞ EVANGELISM: SHARING YOUR STORY AND GOD'S STORY

Goal: To consider how the truths from this lesson might be applied to your relationships with unbelievers

It's very easy for a small group to turn into a clique that only looks inward and loses sight of others outside the group. That's not God's plan. God wants you to reach out to people with his message of love and life change. While this is often scary, this section will give you an opportunity to discuss your relationships with non-Christians and consider ways to listen to their stories, share pieces of your story, and reflect the amazing love of God's story. The icon for this section is a mouth because you're opening your mouth to have spiritual conversations with nonbelievers.

☆ WORSHIP: SURRENDERING YOUR LIFE TO HONOR GOD

Goal: To focus on God's presence

Each session ends with a time of prayer. You'll be challenged to slow down and turn your focus toward God's love, his goodness, and his presence in your life. You'll spend time talking to God, listening in silence, reading Scripture, writing, and focusing on God. The key word for this time is *surrender*, which is giving up what you want so God can give you what he wants. The icon for this section is a body, which represents surrendering your entire life to God.

Oh yeah…there are more sections in each session!

In addition to the main material, there are several additional options you can use to help further and deepen your times with God. Many attend church programs, listen, and then "leave" God until the next week when they return to church. We don't want that to happen to you! So we've provided several more opportunities for you to learn, reflect, and grow on your own.

At the end of every session you'll find three more key headings:

- At Home This Week
- Learn a Little More
- For Further Study

They're fairly easy to figure out, but here's a brief description of each:

AT HOME THIS WEEK

There are five options presented at the end of each session that you can do on your own. They're not homework for the next session (unless your leader assigns them to your group); they're things you can do to keep growing at your own pace. You can skip them, you can do all of them, or you can vary the options from session to session.

Option 1: A Weekly Reflection

At the end of each session you'll find a one-page, quick self-evaluation that helps you reflect on five key areas of your spiritual life (fellowship, discipleship, ministry, evangelism, and worship). It's simply a guide for you to gauge your spiritual health. The first one is on page 32.

Option 2: Daily Bible Readings

One of the challenges in deepening your knowledge of God's Word and learning more about Jesus' life to read the Bible on your own. This option provides a guide to help you read through the Gospel of Mark in 30 days. On page 140 is a list of Bible passages to help you continue to take God's Word deeper into your life.

Option 3: Memory Verses

On page 145 you'll find six Bible verses to memorize. Each is related to the theme of a particular session. (Again, these are optional…remember, nothing is mandatory!)

Option 4: Journaling

You'll find a question or two related to the theme of the session that can serve as a trigger to get you writing. Journaling is a great way to reflect on what you've been learning and evaluate your life. In addition to questions at the end of each section, there's a helpful tool on page 147 that can guide you through the discipline of journaling.

Option 5: Wrap It Up

As you've already read, each session contains too many questions for one small group meeting. So this section provides opportunities to think through your answers to the questions you skipped and then go back and write them down.

LEARN A LITTLE MORE

We've provided some insights (or commentary) on some of the passages that you'll study to help you understand the difficult terms, phrases, and people that you'll read about in each Bible passage.

FOR DEEPER STUDY

One of the best ways to understand the Bible passages and the theme of each session is to dig a little deeper. If deeper study fits your personality style, please use these additional ideas as ways to enhance your learning.

WHAT YOU NEED TO KNOW ABOUT BEING IN A SMALL GROUP

You probably have enough casual or superficial friendships and don't need to waste your time cultivating more. We all need deep and committed friendships. Here are a few ideas to help you benefit the most from your small group time and build great relationships.

Prepare to Participate

Interaction is a key to a good small group. Talking too little will make it hard for others to get to know you. Everyone has something to contribute—yes, even you! But participating doesn't mean dominating, so be careful to not monopolize the conversation! Most groups typically have one conversation hog, and if you don't know who it is in your small group, then it might be you. Here's a tip: You don't have to answer every question and comment on every point. Try to find a balance between the two extremes.

Be Consistent

Healthy relationships take time to grow. Quality time is great, but a great quantity of time is probably better. Commit with your group to show up every week (or whenever your group plans to meet), even when you don't feel like it. With only six sessions per book, if you miss just two meetings you'll have missed a third of what's presented in these pages. When you make a commitment to your small group a high priority, you're sure to build meaningful relationships.

Practice Honesty and Confidentiality

Strong relationships are only as solid as the trust they are built upon. Although it may be difficult, take a risk and be honest with your answers. God wants you to be known by others! Then respect the risks others are taking and offer them the same love, grace, and forgiveness God does. Make confidentiality a nonnegotiable value for your small group. Nothing kills community like gossip.

Arrive Ready to Grow

You can always arrive prepared by praying ahead of time. Ask God to give you the courage to be honest and the discipline to respect others.

You aren't required to do any preparation in the book before you arrive (unless you're the leader—see page 108). If your leader chooses to, she may ask you to do the Disciple-

**Doug Fields &
Brett Eastman**

Doug and Brett were part of the same small group for several years. Brett was the pastor of small groups at Saddleback Church where Doug is the pastor to students. Brett and a team of friends wrote DOING LIFETOGETHER, a group study for adults. Everyone loved it so much that they asked Doug to take the same theme and Bible verses and revise the other material for students. So even though Brett and Doug both had a hand in writing this book, the book you're using is written by Doug—and as a youth pastor, he's cheering you on in your small group experience. For more information on Doug and Brett see page 170.

ship (GROWING) section ahead of time so that you'll have more time to discuss the other sections and make better use of your time.

Congratulations...

...for making a commitment to go through this material with your small group! Life change is within reach when people are united through the same commitment. Your participation in a small group can have a lasting and powerful impact on your life. Our prayer is that the questions and activities in this book help you grow closer to the other group members, and more importantly, to God.

If you're a small group leader, please turn to page 109 for a brief instruction on how best use this material.

SMALL GROUP COVENANT

One of the signs of a healthy small group is that all members understand its purpose. We've learned that members of good small groups make a bond, a commitment, or a covenant to one another.

Read through the following covenant as a group. Be sure to discuss your concerns and questions before you begin your first session. Please feel free to modify the covenant based on the needs and concerns of your particular group. Once you agree with the terms and are willing to commit to the covenant (as you've revised it), sign your own book and have the others sign yours.

With a covenant, your entire group will have the same purpose for your time together, allowing you to grow together and go deeper into your study of God's Word. Without a covenant, groups often find themselves meeting simply for the sake of meeting.

If your group decides to add some additional values, write them at the bottom of the covenant page. Your group may also want to create some rules (such as not interrupting when someone else is speaking or sitting up instead of lying down). You can list those at the bottom of the covenant page also.

Reviewing your group's covenant, values, and rules before each meeting can become a significant part of your small group experience.

A covenant is a binding agreement or contract. God made covenants with Noah, Abraham, and David, among others. Jesus is the fulfillment of a new covenant between God and his people.

SMALL GROUP COVENANT

I, _____, as a member of our small group, acknowledge my need for meaningful relationships with other believers. I agree that this small group community exists to help me deepen my relationships with God, Christians, and other people in my life. I commit to the following:

Consistency

I will give my best effort to attend each of our group meetings.

Honesty

I will take risks to share truthfully about the personal issues in my life.

Confidentiality

I will support the foundation of trust in our small group by not participating in gossip. I will not reveal personal information shared by others during our meetings.

Respect

I will help create a safe environment for our small group members by listening carefully and not making fun of others.

Prayer

I commit to pray regularly for the people in our small group.

Accountability

I will allow the people in my small group to hold me accountable for growing spiritually and living a life that honors God.

This covenant, signed by all the members in this group, reflects our commitment to one another.

Date:

Names:

Additional values our small group members agree to

Additional rules our small group members agree to

JESUS: THE TEACHER

⭐ **LEADERS, READ PAGE 108.**

Justin never really knew his father because he died of cancer when Justin was just three years old. As a teenager, Justin doesn't have many memories of his dad, but he does have a lot of photos and stories that have helped shape his dad's legacy. Because of those photos and stories, Justin has grown up with a desire to be more like his dad.

The stories he's heard over the years make him feel proud that he had such a great dad. His father was a man who followed God's ways, loved his family, and worked hard to make a living. He was adored by many, and everyone describes him to Justin as "one of the greatest guys I've ever met." He was tender, patient, wise, and a great father—and everyone says he loved his son.

Even though his time on earth was short, Justin's dad made a significant impact on others, including Justin. In fact, even though he never knew his dad, Justin's hero is his dad.

As you study the Bible passages in this book and discuss them with your small group, you'll meet (or be reacquainted with) someone you've never seen face-to-face, either, but is more worthy than anyone of hero status—Jesus. You'll learn more about the legacy that Jesus passed on to you. The stories you'll read were written so that as you learn more about Jesus, you'll want to be like Jesus even more.

As you study Jesus with this book, there is an important question you'll want to answer at some point: *Do you really believe Jesus is worth following?* If he's not, you'll keep searching for something or someone to follow. If Jesus is worthy, this study will help you follow him with great enthusiasm, align your life to his teachings, receive his love, and tap into his life-changing power.

This book series, your own study, and your group's discussion will provide chances to look at Jesus in deeper and more meaningful ways—you'll get to know Jesus better! And the great thing about being in a group is that you're not searching, learning, and discovering alone—your group can become an environment where you develop stronger relationships. It's within this group that you'll likely grow, learn, and fall more in love with Jesus. Life isn't meant to be lived alone—doing life together is the way to live it up. Let the journey with Jesus begin!

♥ FELLOWSHIP: CONNECTING YOUR HEART TO OTHERS

Goal: To share about your life and listen attentively to others, caring about what they share

As you study the life of Jesus, you'll notice that people expressed their first impressions of Jesus in different ways. Some were amazed, some afraid, some mad, some confused. You'll develop your own impressions of Jesus as you continue to learn more about him.

Because you're learning in a small group setting, you're

not learning alone. You may already have formed impressions of the other people in your group without knowing much about them. This fellowship section (which is in all six sessions) will provide an opportunity for your group's members to get to know each other better. When you open up a little bit of your life and share pieces of your story, you'll get to know each other better.

Just as the stories of Jesus will give you a clearer picture of him, others' stories will give you a clearer picture of who they really are. To get the most out of this group, it's worth taking a risk and revealing some of yourself and carefully listening to others' hearts. While it can seem scary at first, it does get easier to open up. The benefits of getting to know each other in this way are huge. Be sure to have someone keep an eye on your time in this section, or you may spend your entire time here and not get any further!

Just a reminder: There probably isn't enough time in your small group session to answer every question. Instead choose which ones you'll answer, and then answer the others on your own time. Have fun!

1. Who is one of your current heroes? Why?

2. On a scale of 1 to 10, how much do you think you know about Jesus?

1	2	3	4	5	6	7	8	9	10

Nothing….a little…a little more than a little…some…a lot…no, really a lot…more than my pastor

3. What do want to get out of this small group experience? If your group hasn't discussed the small group covenant on page 18, please take some time now to go through it. Make commitments to each other that your group time will reflect those values (and any additional ones you add). One sign of a healthy small group is that it begins each session by reading the covenant together as a constant reminder of what the group has committed to.

DISCIPLESHIP: GROWING TO BE LIKE JESUS

Goal: To explore God's Word, gain biblical knowledge, and make personal applications

We all have our own understandings of right and wrong—our own systems of values and judgments we consider true. Unfortunately, we often miss the mark with our limited wisdom and believe things are true even when they're not.

For example, as a child I was convinced that chocolate and cookies made a healthy lunch. That was my truth. But I learned actual truth from reliable sources and saw the ignorance of my ways. If you've bought into lies and myths, you need to hear the truth about them.

Jesus spent a lot of time teaching people the truth about God. He taught all kinds of audiences—from gigantic crowds to small groups. He even taught one-on-one to help individuals discover and understand truth. As a teacher, Jesus wasn't interested in just imparting information; rather, he taught to change lives.

Read Mark 1:14-28. (If you don't have a Bible, the passage is on page 113.)

1   According to this passage, what is Jesus teaching?

2. Why do you think Jesus said the "time has come"?

3. In your own words, what does *repent* mean?

4. What is the "good news"? Is there anything from the passage that can help answer this question?

5. In your opinion, what's the connection between "repenting" and "believing the good news"?

6. Why do you think the disciples were so quick to leave their jobs and families behind to follow Jesus?

7. What is the Sabbath? What is a synagogue, and why was Jesus teaching there?

8. According to this passage, what did Jesus do to demonstrate his authority?

9. When did others first recognize his authority? In your opinion, why is this significant?

10. Why is authority important for a teacher? What happens when a teacher lacks authority?

11. Let's get personal: In your opinion, how is it possible to ignore Jesus' teaching when he has authority?

MINISTRY: SERVING OTHERS IN LOVE

Goal: To recognize and take advantage of opportunities to serve others

We don't have the opportunity to do what the first disciples did and follow Jesus around as he taught and cared for people. But you do have the privilege of putting Jesus' teachings into action. One of the major themes of Jesus' life was service. Jesus said, "For even the Son of Man did not come to be served, but to serve, and to give his life as a ransom for many" (Mark 10:45).

In each session you will be given an opportunity to think about service (or ministry), discuss it, or act on it. What you'll learn by serving is that you're never more like Jesus than when you serve.

1   In Mark 1, Jesus not only taught, but he also ministered to the man possessed by an evil spirit. As you continue to study Jesus, you'll see that as he taught he also served and cared for the needs of others. What needs do you think Jesus—and you—would see if you walked through the following environments in your own life? List a few needs under each one.

Your City:

Your Campus:

Your Home:

Underline one of these needs you just wrote down; that's the need you will try to meet this week. Tell your group which one you underlined. (These needs don't have to be newsworthy. You don't need to build a house! The goal isn't getting on the front page of the paper; it's developing your heart for serving others…just like Jesus.)

2.   If you do meet a need this week, come back to this space and write down (a) specifically what you did, (b) what you learned, and (c) how you felt. Be prepared to share your experience the next time your group meets.

EVANGELISM: SHARING YOUR STORY AND GOD'S STORY

Goal: To consider how the truths from this lesson might be applied to your relationships with unbelievers

When Jesus called his disciples away from the fishing boat, he said he would make them fishers of men. He used their profession—what they already knew how to do—and connected it with evangelism.

1.   In the same way, what could you envision Jesus using from your life—a hobby, sports team, workplace? Where are you involved with others? How might Jesus connect your interests to evangelism? Don't be afraid to laugh at some of the ideas—they may be funny.

2.   Based on what you've studied today, how would Jesus respond to unbelievers? What message do you think he would want them to hear about the kind of teacher he is?

3.   Do you feel comfortable sharing that message? Why, or why not?

It's vital for your group to decide at this first session whether you can invite friends to join your group. Talk about the structure of your group and stick to your decision. If you decide the answer is no, you may be able to invite friends to join you in the next EXPERIENCING CHRIST TOGETHER book—there are six of them, so there's plenty of time! If you're a small group leader, see the Small Group Leader Checklist on page 108.

🚶 WORSHIP: SURRENDERING YOUR LIFE TO HONOR GOD

Goal: To focus on God's presence

According to the Scriptures, when Jesus called the fishermen to become his followers, they left "at once" and "immediately." Those are words that describe a powerful response to a personal call.

You'll find three prayer resources in the appendices in the back of this book. By reading them (and possibly discussing them), you'll find your group prayer time more rewarding.
• Praying in Your Small Group (page 156). Read this article on your own before the next session.
• Prayer Request Guidelines (page 158). Read and discuss these guidelines as a group.
• Prayer Options (page 160). Refer to this list for ideas to add variety to your prayer time.

1. You may have read the passage from another Bible translation. What other words are used to describe how the fishermen responded to Jesus' call to follow him?

2. What phrase best describes your reaction to following Jesus and his ways? Circle one, and explain why in the space below.

    - I, too, followed immediately!
    - I asked a lot of questions before I left my old ways to follow Jesus.
    - I haven't left my old ways yet.
    - Jesus who?
    - I followed Jesus because others followed.
    - I followed Jesus when I was younger, but I've since returned to my old ways.
    - Other:

3. Take one minute of silence and really think about what you would do if Jesus looked you in the eyes and said, "Follow me." Share your response.

Small group sessions will usually end with prayer. This is your opportunity to talk to God and tell him what's on your heart and ask for his help to follow his ways so you can become more like Jesus.

If your small group is new, don't feel pressured to have everyone pray out loud if they're not comfortable. Group members can pray in silence, and God hears those prayers too.

AT HOME THIS WEEK

One of the consistent values of our LIFETOGETHER books is that we want you to have options for growing spiritually on your own during the week. To help with this "on your own" value, we'll give you five options. If you do these, you'll have more to contribute when you return to your small group, and you'll begin to develop spiritual habits that can last your entire life. Here are the five you'll see after every section. (You might try to do one per day on the days after your small group meets.)

Option 1: A Weekly Reflection

After each session you'll find a quick, one-page self-evaluation that reflects the five areas of your spiritual life found in this book (fellowship, discipleship, ministry, evangelism, and worship). After each evaluation, you decide if there's anything you'll do differently with your life. This page is all for you. It's not intended as a report card that you turn into your small group leader. The first evaluation is on page 32.

Option 2: Daily Bible Readings

On page 140 you'll find a list of Bible passages that will help you read through an entire book of the Bible in 30 days. If you choose this option, try to read one of the assigned passages each day. Highlight key verses in your Bible, reflect on them, journal about them, or write down any questions you have from your reading. We want to encourage you to take time to read God's love letter—the Bible. You'll find helpful tips in "How to Study the Bible On Your Own" (page 142).

Option 3: Memory Verses

Of the five options listed here, mark the option(s) that seem most appealing to you. Share with your group the one(s) you plan to do in the upcoming week. This helps you keep one another accountable as you continue to study and grow on your own.

Memorizing Bible verses is an important habit to develop as you learn to grow spiritually on your own. "Memory Verses" (page 145) contains six verses for you to memorize—one per session. Memorizing verses (and making them stick for more than a few minutes) isn't easy, but the benefits are undeniable. You'll have God's Word with you wherever you go.

> **"I HAVE HIDDEN YOUR WORD IN MY HEART THAT I MIGHT NOT SIN AGAINST YOU."**
> **(PSALM 119:11)**

Option 4: Journaling

You'll find blank pages for journaling beginning on page 150. At the end of each session, you'll find questions to get your thoughts going—but you aren't limited to answering the questions listed. Use these pages to reflect, write a letter to God, note what you're learning, compose prayer, ask questions, draw pictures, record your thoughts, or take notes if your small group is using the EXPERIENCING CHRIST TOGETHER DVD teachings. For some suggestions about journaling, turn to "Journaling: Snapshots of Your Heart" on page 147.

For this session, choose one or more of the following questions to kickstart your journaling:

- I'm excited to be in a group because...
- If someone asked me to describe Jesus, I would say...
- Jesus as a teacher would want me to know...

Option 5: Wrap It Up

Go back through the session and answer the questions your group didn't have time to discuss.

LEARN A LITTLE MORE

Goal: To help you better understand the Scripture passage you studied in this session by highlighting key words and other important information

After John was put in prison (Mark 1:14)

John the Baptist was Jesus' cousin. John's ministry prepared people for Jesus (see Mark 1-8). Jesus would face the same fate as John and be handed over to the authorities for a death sentence (Mark 15:15).

The kingdom of God (1:15)

This describes a kingdom in which God's way dominates (Matthew 6:10). It will be a kingdom of goodness, joy, and beauty. Our planet withdrew from God's kingdom when humans (whom God had put in charge) rebelled against God's ways (see the beginning chapters of Genesis). The Bible tells us that God desires to bring us back into his kingdom.

God created the nation of Israel (the Jewish people) to be a gathering place of his kingdom, to attract the rest of humanity to join his kingdom. As the Bible teaches in the Old Testament, Israel repeatedly failed to obey God's ways and commands. As a result, God allowed different empires to oppress them. By Jesus' birth, the Roman Empire dominated the people of Israel. Many Jews were desperate for a leader who would throw out the Romans and restore God's kingdom on earth, both politically and spiritually. The Bible contains many prophecies about a leader who would be called the Messiah (the Hebrew word for "anointed one"; the Greek word for messiah is *Christ*). Jewish history records several self-proclaimed messiahs, but none brought the kind of change the Jews were looking for.

Jesus is the prophesied Messiah, and God's kingdom was the central message of his teaching. But Jesus had no intention of being a military Messiah and destroying the Romans to establish a political kingdom. Instead he invited everyone to stop pursuing their own agendas and rejoin God's kingdom. God's kingdom was (and is) immediately available to anyone who followed Jesus. But only in part. Jesus will ultimately bring his kingdom in all its fullness when he returns.

Repent (1:15)

In the language of the New Testament, this word means "to change your mind" or to think about things in a radically different way. A related Hebrew word for repent means to change course or to look for what you need by going in a completely different direction.

Fishers of men (1:17)

The Greek word for men in this verse is anthropos and refers to all people, both men and women.

Galilee...Capernaum (1:14,21)

Galilee is the region where Jesus did most of his ministry. Capernaum is a town on the Sea of Galilee, home to both Peter and Andrew (two of Jesus' disciples).

Sabbath (1:21)

God created the earth in seven days; he worked for six and rested (literally, he "ceased") on the seventh day. God did this as a model for us to follow. He certainly doesn't need the rest, but we do! The idea of the Sabbath is for people to stop and take a "time out" from our busy lives to refocus on God. For many Jews, the Sabbath is a celebration, spent in prayer and with family. Out of a misguided desire to observe the Sabbath as God intended, the religious leaders of Jesus' day created many rules governing human conduct on the Sabbath. These detailed rules started with Scripture but were closer to human tradition than God's revelation.

Synagogue (1:21)

The synagogue is a place where local groups of Jewish people assemble for worship, prayer, and instruction in the Law of

Moses. The main meeting day is on the Jewish Sabbath (Saturday). Typical meetings include recited prayers and a reading from the Scriptures, followed by an explanation or sermon. The synagogue is also a center for community activities not directly related to worship and prayer.

Originally, the primary place of worship for the Jews was at the temple in Jerusalem. During their exile from their land and captivity by the Babylonians (which began in 586 B.C.), the synagogue arose as a new place of worship, serving as an alternative to the temple that was now out of reach.

Teachers of the Law (1:22)

These teachers were also known as "scribes." Although portrayed as a unified group, the New Testament doesn't provide much detail about their distinctive characteristics. Based on their portrayal in the Gospels, "They were the scholars of the day, professionally trained in the interpretation and application of the Law. Jesus often came into direct conflict with them."

FOR DEEPER STUDY ON YOUR OWN

1. Read the surrounding context of this passage for better understanding (Mark 1:1-28). Make a list of recurring themes or words you find in this passage.

2. The Sermon on the Mount is arguably Jesus' most famous teaching. Read Matthew 5-7 and note anything that stands out to you.

3. Isaiah 50:4-11 is an Old Testament portrait of a disciple. Jesus lived this way. What features of this portrait seem most significant to you?

A WEEKLY REFLECTION

Take a minute to reflect on how well you've been doing in the following five areas of your spiritual life this week—a 10 means you were amazing. This reflection can serve as a spiritual gauge to help you consider some very important areas. This is for your personal evaluation and growth; it's NOT a test—no one else needs to see it.

FELLOWSHIP: CONNECTING YOUR HEART TO OTHERS'

How well did I connect with other Christians?

1   2   3   4   5   6   7   8   9   10

DISCIPLESHIP: GROWING TO BE LIKE JESUS

How well did I take steps to grow spiritually and deepen my faith on my own?

1   2   3   4   5   6   7   8   9   10

MINISTRY: SERVING OTHERS IN LOVE

How well did I recognize opportunities to serve others and follow through?

1   2   3   4   5   6   7   8   9   10

EVANGELISM: SHARING YOUR STORY AND GOD'S STORY

How well did I engage in spiritual conversations with non-Christians?

1   2   3   4   5   6   7   8   9   10

WORSHIP: SURRENDERING YOUR LIFE TO HONOR GOD

How well did I focus on God's presence and honor him with my life? Was my relationship with God a primary focus?

1   2   3   4   5   6   7   8   9   10

When you finish, celebrate the areas where you feel good and consider how you can use those strengths to help others in their journey to be more like Jesus. You might also want to take time to identify some potential areas for growth.

JESUS: THE HEALER

⭐ **LEADERS, READ PAGE 108.**

Kyle attended church camp over the summer, but he had a terrible attitude about it. He kept himself disconnected from others and appeared tired all the time. He was only there because his parents forced him to go, and he didn't want anything to do with the God-thing. So he decided to run away from home the night he returned from camp. That would show his parents! He knew they loved him, but he didn't think they understood—or even tried to understand—him. Running away from home seemed a sensible solution for this hopeless situation.

One night at camp, Kyle casually mentioned his runaway plans to some of the guys in his cabin. They didn't respond casually. Instead, they aggressively committed to step into Kyle's life and help him with his struggles. Throughout the remainder of the week, they gathered at night with Kyle to talk and pray and share their own struggles. By the last night of camp, Kyle didn't feel so alone and even began to imagine what his life could be like if he asked Jesus to change his life like the guys in his cabin had.

During the times of connection with his new friends, Kyle felt as if God was actually healing him of his hopelessness. God used camp and Kyle's new friends to change him. He returned home and told his parents about his struggles and how he wanted things to change. He told them he had made a commitment to follow the teachings of Jesus and establish a personal relationship with God. He did the possible at camp and prayed that God would do the impossible in his life.

God came through! He began to heal Kyle's heart and help restore the relationship with his family. It's not a perfect relationship today, but it's a lot better than it was because Kyle allowed God to play a role in his life.

In this session you're going to look at Jesus as the healer. He brought healing to Kyle, and he's an expert at what you think is impossible.

♥ FELLOWSHIP: CONNECTING YOUR HEART TO OTHERS

Goal: To share about your life and listen attentively to others, caring about what they share

As you get started, you can choose to either check in with each other to see if anyone did a SERVING project from Session 1 (see page 23) and talk about your experiences, or you can answer the following questions.

1. If you could be healed of anything right now, what would it be?

2. Jesus brought physical healing to many people. Do you believe that type of physical healing is possible today? What about other kinds of healing—spiritual, emotional, or mental healing?

DISCIPLESHIP: GROWING TO BE LIKE JESUS

Goal: To explore God's Word, gain biblical knowledge, and make personal applications

Everywhere Jesus went he made a huge difference in people's lives. His teaching softened hearts and expanded minds. But he also offered forgiveness—and that lifted unbearable guilt and brought personal healing and spiritual revival to many. His display of miracles shouted to the world that he was divine. And because Jesus shared God's nature, he had all of God's power to heal at his disposal.

Jesus was the master at helping people where they needed it most, and even though his purpose was to restore people to God (heal them spiritually), he often met their physical needs as well. Here are two examples. (Read both accounts if you have time or study one as a group and the other by yourself when you're at home this week.)

Read Mark 1:40-45. **(If you don't have a Bible, the passage is on page 113.)**

1. Why do you think the leper says, "If you are willing?" Wouldn't Jesus always be willing to help someone?

2. If God loves everyone so much, why do you think he hasn't healed everyone—or at least all Christians?

3. At first it might seem strange that Jesus told the healed leper to say nothing to anyone. According to the text, what was the result of the man speaking freely?

4. In this passage, the healed leper disobeyed Jesus by telling others what Jesus had done for him, but he spoke the truth. Was this unwise? Can you think of any present-day examples of this from your own life? What happened?

   If something is true, should you be able to communicate it however you want...even if it disobeys God's direction?

   Are there any examples from your life where you disobeyed some of God's instructions found in the Bible and later discovered that God was right and you were wrong?

5. Why do you think Jesus told the man to offer the sacrifices Moses commanded? Were sacrifices still necessary? (You may want to read the study notes on page 45 for help.)

Read Mark 2:1-12. (**If you don't have a Bible, the passage is on page 114.**)

6. Why do you think the house was so full of people?

7. What role does faith play in this passage? What was more important, the faith of the individual or the faith of the group?

8. Why did Jesus forgive the paralytic's sins before healing him? Why not the other way around?

9. In your own words, what is blasphemy? How does this Bible passage help answer this question?

10. Why were the teachers of the law so angered by what Jesus did?

11. What does this event teach about Jesus' nature? Why is this significant?

12. Why do you think Jesus didn't have the paralytic stay and listen to the rest of his teaching?

    a. Healing was more important than teaching.
    b. He was whole and didn't need to take up space in a crowded room.
    c. He was healed and needed to leave to celebrate.
    d. Other:

13. Consider your own spiritual life right now. Who do you identify with the most in this event?

    a. the HURTING paralytic on the mat
    b. one of the four FAITHFUL friends
    c. the CRITICAL religious leaders

MINISTRY: SERVING OTHERS IN LOVE

Goal: To recognize and take advantage of opportunities to serve others

1. Can you imagine yourself participating in a ministry to people who are sick, hospitalized, or unable to care for themselves? If yes, how? If not, why not?

Where are some opportunities for this kind of service in your community?

2. How might a small group of teenagers do something to help them? Is there a group from your church already doing something for these people that you could join?

EVANGELISM: SHARING YOUR STORY AND GOD'S STORY

Goal: To consider how the truths from this lesson might be applied to your relationships with unbelievers

1. If you were in the crowd and had seen Jesus heal the leper or the paralytic, how do you think that would affect your desire to tell others about Jesus?

2. Would evangelism be easier if we could heal everyone with a problem? In your opinion, should God give every Christian the ability to heal so we could share our faith more effectively?

3. Read the following passage out loud and then answer the questions below.

While Jesus was having dinner at Levi's house, many tax collectors and "sinners" were eating with him and his disciples, for there were many who followed him. When the teachers of the law who were Pharisees saw him eating with the "sinners" and tax collectors, they asked his disciples: "Why does he eat with tax collectors and 'sinners'?" On hearing this, Jesus said to them, "It is not the healthy who need a doctor, but the sick. I have not come to call the righteous, but sinners." (Mark 2:15-17)

As your group stays together, it can be really easy to have a good group turn negative and become a clique. Don't allow this to happen. You might all commit to reading "How to Keep Your Small Group from Becoming a Clique" before the next time you get together. It's on page 129.

Is your church and/or youth group a place where "the sick" feel comfortable attending?

How might your youth group become a place where they feel welcome?

4. Think of one friend who doesn't know Jesus. Now, like the friends of the paralytic in Mark 2, how might you help your friend overcome obstacles and come to a place where she can encounter Jesus? Does she need a ride to church? Questions answered? How can you serve her?

🚶 WORSHIP: SURRENDERING YOUR LIFE TO HONOR GOD

Goal: To focus on God's presence

Jesus wants to be present in your life and in your group as the Healer. End your time together by sharing how you would like to experience healing (spiritually, physically, emotionally, or mentally). You might want to consider writing down the healing prayer requests on page 162. Close by praying for one another.

AT HOME THIS WEEK

Option 1: A Weekly Reflection

Take another self-evaluation that reflects five areas of your spiritual life (fellowship, discipleship, ministry, evangelism, worship). See page 46.

Option 2: Daily Bible Readings

Check out the Bible reading plan on page 140.

Option 3: Memory Verses

Memorize another verse from page 145.

Option 4: Journaling

Choose one or more of the following options:

- Write down whatever is on your mind.
- Read your journal entry from last week and write a reflection about it.
- Respond to these questions: Was I completely honest with my group about my need for healing? What do I really want to be healed of? Why was I afraid to share it with the group?

Option 5: Wrap It Up

Write out your answers to any questions that you didn't answer during your small group time.

LEARN A LITTLE MORE

Goal: To help you better understand the Scripture passage you studied in this session by highlighting key words and other important information

Leprosy (Mark 1:40)

The definition of this term includes a wide variety of skin diseases. These were not only physical diseases (sometimes horribly painful and disfiguring), but at the time they were also "social diseases." Many skin diseases are contagious, and lepers in Jesus' time were isolated from others and treated poorly. Because people feared contact with them, lepers became outcasts. Many lepers were considered "unclean" for worship in the temple (Leviticus 13:45-46). For a rabbi like Jesus to touch a leper was revolutionary.

Don't tell this to anyone (1:44)

Sometimes Jesus did miracles publicly, but other times he healed people privately and asked them not to tell others about what he had done. He may have wanted to keep the masses from proclaiming him the Messiah until he'd had time to demonstrate what kind of Messiah he was. (Do you remember this from Session 1?) While people expected a military Messiah, Jesus' mission was to overthrow sin and eternal separation from God through his death on the cross.

Also Jesus avoided self-promotion that would make him a mere celebrity (John 7:1-8). Instead, he carefully chose moments for public acknowledgement (John 7:14,37-44). His priority was preaching the good news of God's kingdom. Before healing the leper in this passage, Jesus was able to heal lepers freely in the town synagogues throughout Galilee—but after the leper spread news of this miracle, Jesus was swamped with crowds wanting more miracles, hindering his preaching ministry (Mark 1:45).

Offer the sacrifices (1:44)

The Law of Moses required that once a person was cured of an infectious skin disease, he needed to worship God by offering sacrifices. After the sacrifices were offered, the priest would then declare the person clean. (See Leviticus 14:2-32 for the details of this ceremony.)

Sins (2:5)

Sin is disobeying God's direct commands outlined in Exodus 20:1-17 and restated in Matthew 5:21-48. At the highest level, sin is a failure to obey perfectly the great commandments of loving God and others. It's not trying to follow God's ways and falling just a little short—it's complete failure.

Blasphemy (2:7)

Blasphemy means speaking against God and teaching lies about his character and nature. Jesus claimed to be God, equal in power and authority. Because the Jewish religious leaders didn't believe him, they charged him with blasphemy and handed Jesus over to the Romans for execution (Mark 14:64).

Who can forgive sins but God alone? (2:7)

Consider how sin and forgiveness work. First, when we harm another person, we sin against that person. When we do what we want rather than what God wants, we sin against God. Therefore, all sin is ultimately against God (in addition to others harmed). Second, the only person who can forgive sin is the one who was harmed. For example, you can't forgive your neighbor's friend for crashing your neighbor's car. It's none of your business. But since ultimately God is the owner of the life we have hurt by sin, God is the only one who has the right to issue forgiveness in our lives.

FOR DEEPER STUDY ON YOUR OWN

1. Check out the following healings Jesus performed: Matthew 9:27-34; Luke 7:1-10, 17:11-19.

2. Healing played a part in the ministry of some of the earlier prophets (2 Kings 4:1-37, 5:1-14). How was Jesus' healing ministry similar to theirs? How was it different?

A WEEKLY REFLECTION

Take a minute to reflect on how well you've been doing in the following five areas of your spiritual life this week—a 10 means you were amazing. This reflection can serve as a spiritual gauge to help you consider some very important areas. This is for your personal evaluation and growth; it's NOT a test—no one else needs to see it.

FELLOWSHIP: CONNECTING YOUR HEART TO OTHERS'

How well did I connect with other Christians?

1   2   3   4   5   6   7   8   9   10

DISCIPLESHIP: GROWING TO BE LIKE JESUS

How well did I take steps to grow spiritually and deepen my faith on my own?

1   2   3   4   5   6   7   8   9   10

MINISTRY: SERVING OTHERS IN LOVE

How well did I recognize opportunities to serve others and follow through?

1   2   3   4   5   6   7   8   9   10

EVANGELISM: SHARING YOUR STORY AND GOD'S STORY

How well did I engage in spiritual conversations with non-Christians?

1   2   3   4   5   6   7   8   9   10

WORSHIP: SURRENDERING YOUR LIFE TO HONOR GOD

How well did I focus on God's presence and honor him with my life? Was my relationship with God a primary focus?

1   2   3   4   5   6   7   8   9   10

When you finish, celebrate the areas where you feel good and consider how you can use those strengths to help others in their journey to be more like Jesus. You might also want to take time to identify some potential areas for growth.

JESUS: THE SHEPHERD

★ LEADERS, READ PAGE 108.

Hilary's teenage years were a season of experimenting, testing, and deciding what was worth living for. Although she had committed her life to Jesus when she was a little girl, she wandered away from God, church, and the friends who really loved her when she entered high school. She was drawn toward what she thought were "greener pastures." She spent a lot of her teenage years seeking happiness from parties and relationships instead of living God's way.

Despite walking away from God, Hilary experienced God's love through the people she encountered. Christians continually reached out to include her, inviting her to church, Bible studies, and Christ-centered events. Time after time, Jesus protected her from the harm that showed up around every party corner. God never stopped pursuing Hilary and loving her. After many invitations, she finally returned to the life she was meant to live, with the people who cared for her and to the God who never stopped loving her.

When someone goes his own way, it breaks God's heart. As you go through this session, you'll want to take note of the biblical truth that God wants the very best for you. Even if you decide to go your own way, God is still crazy about you and will never withhold his love from you. As you study the caring heart of Jesus the Shepherd, consider that his heart is the same heart that God has for you!

♥ FELLOWSHIP: CONNECTING YOUR HEART TO OTHERS

Goal: To share about your life and listen attentively to others, caring about what they share

During this session, you're going to take a look at another description of Jesus: the Good Shepherd. This could be a bit of a foreign term to most of us since so few people today have had experience with shepherding. But when you understand what Jesus came to do (and wants to do in your life today)—and then learn what a shepherd's job is—you'll better understand and appreciate Jesus as Shepherd.

1. What is a shepherd's primary role? (You might want to read "What's a Shepherd?" on page 58 and then answer the question.)

2. Why do sheep need a shepherd? (You might want to read "Stupid Sheep" on page 57.)

3. Thinking about what you've learned about a shepherd's job, answer these questions:

   Who in your life cares for you, guides you, and looks out for your best interests?

   What is your relationship like with that person?

DISCIPLESHIP: GROWING TO BE LIKE JESUS

Goal: To explore God's Word, gain biblical knowledge, and make personal applications

Jesus used the powerful image of a shepherd to describe himself because it strikes at the core of what people need most: to be included, wanted, known by name, protected, and guided—essentially to be cared for completely by a loving God. God's love is so wonderful because it connects to the deepest parts of who you are. Jesus the Shepherd cares for you and wants to meet all your needs.

Read John 10:1-5. (If you don't have a Bible, the passage is on page 114.)

1. Explain this figure of speech in your own words. What is the relationship between the shepherd and his sheep?

2. This passage highlights the need for direction and guidance from a shepherd. Do you feel like you follow Jesus?

   What are some things in your life that keep you from following Jesus as shepherd?

3. In these verses, the sheep run from the stranger because they do not recognize his voice. What does this mean for people following Jesus as their shepherd?

4. For you personally, what does it mean to know the voice of Jesus?

How can you tell the difference between the shepherd's voice and a stranger's (or thief's)?

Read John 10:6-10.

5. Why do you think Jesus first calls himself the shepherd (verses 1-5) and then the gate?

6. These verses highlight the need for protection from thieves. What is the difference between the thief and Jesus?

How have you experienced these differences in your own life?

7. Jesus said that he came to give us life in all its fullness (verse 10). What's the difference between a life before Jesus entered it and a life of fullness following him?

Do you feel like you are experiencing life in all its fullness? If not, why not?

Read John 10:11-18.

8. Now Jesus introduces a new character: the "hired hand." What is the main difference between the shepherd and the hired hand?

9. In this passage, what two things does the Good Shepherd do for his sheep? Why are they significant?

10. These three passages put together (John 10:1-18) highlight three different needs we all share:

    a. The need for direction and purpose
    b. The need for protection from harm
    c. The need to know God better

    Which of these three is currently your biggest need?

11. Because the Good Shepherd laid down his life for us, we can have a relationship with God. In this passage, people are divided into those who know the shepherd and those who don't. Do you know God in the way this passage describes? Explain your answer.

MINISTRY: SERVING OTHERS IN LOVE

Goal: To recognize and take advantage of opportunities to serve others

Now that you know the primary role of a shepherd, you can better answer these questions.

1. Do you believe you have what it takes to play a shepherd-like role in a younger Christian's life? Why, or why not?

2. What do you need to do in order to move from "That sounds like a good idea" to "I can shepherd someone, and I will"?

3. How might it change your youth group (or small group) if each person in the group were to care for (shepherd) younger students in your church? How would this serve others?

EVANGELISM: SHARING YOUR STORY AND GOD'S STORY

Goal: To consider how the truths from this lesson might be applied to your relationships with unbelievers

1. What is attractive about Jesus as Shepherd? Make a list below:

2. Name some of your non-Christian friends' needs that Jesus (as their Shepherd) could meet.

3. How might you communicate the connection between your list (#1) and their needs (#2)?

4. Do you think everyone needs the life described in John 10:10?

What can you do to make this life attractive for non-Christians in your life?

WORSHIP: SURRENDERING YOUR LIFE TO HONOR GOD

Goal: To focus on God's presence

1. Have one person read Psalm 23 out loud. (If you don't have a Bible, the passage is on pages 115-116.)

2. Now have a different person read it aloud. This time write down any words that strike you as important.

3. Based on what you learned in this session and what you heard during the readings of Psalm 23, paraphrase Psalm 23 (using as much of your own vocabulary as possible).

If you have time and if you feel comfortable, share what you wrote.

4. Close your time together by praying and thanking God for the specific ways he shepherds you.

Leaders: You may want to read the worship section in Session 4 (page 69) before your next meeting. The next time you meet, the group will discuss Jesus as servant, and there's a potential activity that will require some extra work before you meet again.

Take some time on your own this week to answer the questions from the Spiritual Health Assessment (page 131). The goal is to evaluate your spiritual life in an honest way—you're not out for a high score, but honesty. You may have the opportunity to share your results during your next session.

AT HOME THIS WEEK

Option 1: A Weekly Reflection

Take another self-evaluation that reflects five areas of your spiritual life (fellowship, discipleship, ministry, evangelism, worship). See page 60.

Option 2: Daily Bible Readings

Check out the Bible reading plan on page 140.

Option 3: Memory Verses

Memorize another verse from page 145.

Option 4: Journaling

Choose one or more of the following options:

- Write down whatever is on your mind.
- Read your journal entry from last week and write a reflection about it.
- Respond to this question: What do you personally need from Jesus the Shepherd?

Option 5: Wrap It Up

Write out your answers to any questions that you didn't answer during your small group time.

LEARN A LITTLE MORE

Goal: To help you better understand the Scripture passage you studied in this session by highlighting key words and other important information

"Stupid Sheep"

Sheep and shepherds were common sights in Jesus' day. Sheep were neither strong enough nor smart enough to survive the often-harsh Middle Eastern environment on their own. Without the constant care of a shepherd, sheep die from thirst, bad water, cold, wolf attacks, or just from falling over and having too much bulk to stand up. Plus, they tend to wander away and get lost. (They're not the smartest animals. Have you ever seen one in a circus?)

"What's a Shepherd?"

"From earliest times the work of shepherding was…very important. Since the shepherd had to feed as well as protect the flock, he traveled some distance, especially in the hot summer period. Each night he counted the sheep into an open fold, and he would lie across the opening, so becoming the 'door of the sheep.' He had to keep a keen watch for the wild animals that came up from the tangled 'jungle' of the Jordan Valley—including lions, in Old Testament times, and jackals. The shepherd usually had charge of a mixed flock of sheep and goats. He could drive the goats, but he led the sheep."[1]

All who ever came before me were thieves and robbers (John 10:8)

This is perhaps a specific reference to Jewish religious leaders and describes those interested only in themselves, not about the sheep's well being. If we correctly understand the word *before* within the context of these verses, then any person who came to the sheep *before* the shepherd would be coming during the night—and probably not with good intentions. (In contrast, the shepherd comes to his sheep early in the morning to care for them.) Whoever Jesus is specifically referring to in this verse is not a major issue; the point is that anyone who claims to offer life apart from Jesus is nothing but a robber and a thief.

I have come that they may have life, and have it to the full (10:10)

Some translations use the word abundant in this verse. Full means beyond measure, over and above, more than necessary, surpassing. Life that good only comes from the Good Shepherd. We often miss out on all that Jesus has for us when we fail to see him as our shepherd—when we don't hear his voice or follow his lead to the abundant life he has for us.

[1.] D. Alexander, editor, *Eerdmans Handbook to the Bible* (Grand Rapids, Mich.: Eerdmans, 1973), p. 93.

I have other sheep that are not of this sheep pen...and there shall be one flock and one shepherd (10:16)

This verse has led to some confusing teachings over the years. Jesus refers here to followers who were unknown to Jesus' disciples but clearly known by God. There's one example of this in Mark's Gospel:

> "TEACHER," SAID JOHN, "WE SAW A MAN DRIVING OUT DEMONS IN YOUR NAME AND WE TOLD HIM TO STOP, BECAUSE HE WAS NOT ONE OF US." "DO NOT STOP HIM," JESUS SAID. "NO ONE WHO DOES A MIRACLE IN MY NAME CAN IN THE NEXT MOMENT SAY ANYTHING BAD ABOUT ME, FOR WHOEVER IS NOT AGAINST US IS FOR US." (MARK 9:38-40)

It seems as though John had a limited perspective while Jesus had a handle on the big picture. Another example of this can be found in the prophet Elisha, who was convinced he was the last of God's people (1 Kings 19:10). But he, too, had a limited perspective. In his case, God knew more than 7,000 faithful people (1 Kings 19:18).

In the John passage that you studied, "not of this sheep pen" may be a reference to Gentile (non-Jewish) believers. While we might not know exactly *who* Jesus is referring to (other than the fact that they were unknown to the disciples), it's clear from this passage that they will someday be part of the one flock under the Good Shepherd.

I lay down my life—only to take it up again (10:17)

Sheep were protected at all costs and needed that protection because they weren't (and still aren't) very smart. The ultimate test of a shepherd was his willingness to lay down his life for his sheep (1 Samuel 17:34-36). Jesus is that kind of shepherd for you. He willingly laid down his life on the cross for your sake, demonstrating his sacrificial love.

FOR DEEPER STUDY ON YOUR OWN

1. How does Jesus further use the shepherd image to explain his own mission and the Father's heart? (See Luke 15:1-7.)

2. Read Ezekiel 34 to see shepherd imagery used in the Old Testament. How does this compare with what you've read in the New Testament?

3. Read 1 Peter 5:1-4. How does Peter use the same image when he instructs leaders and members of the early church?

A WEEKLY REFLECTION

Take a minute to reflect on how well you've been doing in the following five areas of your spiritual life this week—a 10 means you were amazing. This reflection can serve as a spiritual gauge to help you consider some very important areas. This is for your personal evaluation and growth; it's NOT a test—no one else needs to see it.

FELLOWSHIP: CONNECTING YOUR HEART TO OTHERS'

How well did I connect with other Christians?

1 2 3 4 5 6 7 8 9 10

DISCIPLESHIP: GROWING TO BE LIKE JESUS

How well did I take steps to grow spiritually and deepen my faith on my own?

1 2 3 4 5 6 7 8 9 10

MINISTRY: SERVING OTHERS IN LOVE

How well did I recognize opportunities to serve others and follow through?

1 2 3 4 5 6 7 8 9 10

EVANGELISM: SHARING YOUR STORY AND GOD'S STORY

How well did I engage in spiritual conversations with non-Christians?

1 2 3 4 5 6 7 8 9 10

WORSHIP: SURRENDERING YOUR LIFE TO HONOR GOD

How well did I focus on God's presence and honor him with my life? Was my relationship with God a primary focus?

1 2 3 4 5 6 7 8 9 10

When you finish, celebrate the areas where you feel good and consider how you can use those strengths to help others in their journey to be more like Jesus. You might also want to take time to identify some potential areas for growth.

SESSION 4

JESUS: THE SERVANT

⭐ **LEADERS, READ PAGE 108.**

Scott was having a hard time with math. He would figure out one problem—then discover he was still three problems behind everybody else. He knew math was going to be a killer for him!

Scott enjoyed his small group at church, and he had a good relationship with everyone except the new kid, Brandon. He just didn't know him very well yet. When Brandon mentioned something about math being his favorite subject, Scott immediately thought, "Score! I'll get to know the new kid." After the small group, Scott asked Brandon to tutor him. Brandon was eager to make a new friend, but he had an after-school job and wasn't available to tutor Scott until after 9 p.m. The late time didn't matter to Scott—he was desperate enough to get help at midnight! Arrangements were made, and the following night Scott drove to what he thought was Brandon's house. But instead of a house, he found himself pulling up to an old, rundown motel.

He thought he'd made a mistake, but he knocked on the door anyway. Brandon answered.

Scott and Brandon didn't get to math that night. Brandon told Scott how his dad had lost his job, forcing their family of five to move into cheap housing. Brandon worked at a grocery store every day to help with the family finances—and to get a discount on groceries.

Suddenly Scott's math problems seemed insignificant. His heart broke for Brandon. He couldn't believe something like this was happening to a guy his own age. But what could he do? Brandon and his family had a huge need, way too big for one teenager to fix. He offered to drive Brandon to school and work so he didn't have to walk. It wasn't much, but it was all he could think of doing in an attempt to help. He'd have to make a few minor sacrifices to make it happen, but it was nothing in comparison to Brandon's sacrifices to help his family survive.

Helping Brandon turned out to be an amazing experience for Scott that year. He made a lifelong friend, helped a Christian brother in a very practical way, and eventually—with Brandon's expert help—passed his math class with a B-.

In this session you will find out what it means to be a servant like Jesus as you begin to consider how you can serve those around you.

♥ FELLOWSHIP: CONNECTING YOUR HEART TO OTHERS

Goal: To share about your life and listen attentively to others, caring about what they share

1. Share with the group about your favorite personal space. This is the spot where you feel most comfortable, safe, and warm. This could be your bedroom, a favorite chair in your house, the front seat of your car, your garage, or a booth at a coffee shop.

What makes this space your favorite?

2. How would you feel if you had to give up your favorite space to someone in need? In what ways, if any, would it be difficult to do? Be honest—it's okay if it's difficult. You're normal!

DISCIPLESHIP: GROWING TO BE LIKE JESUS

Goal: To explore God's Word, gain biblical knowledge, and make personal applications

Jesus didn't come to earth to be served; he came to serve the world so we can be in relationship with God (Mark 10:45). Jesus' servanthood wasn't comfortable, nice, or convenient. It wasn't the kind of service that gained him popularity—it led him to death. Jesus' servanthood was so radical that it was even misunderstood by his closest followers. Jesus served to show us the full extent of his love. It's this kind of servant-hood that we are called to imitate.

Read John 13:1-17. (If you don't have a Bible, the passage is on page 116.)

1. Why is it sometimes difficult to serve and help others? Think about your own experiences—what keeps you from serving?

2. How do you think Jesus felt as he washed his disciples' feet? Do you think it was difficult for him?

3. Peter was shocked that Jesus wanted to wash his feet. Can you think of people in your life who'd be shocked by your desire to serve them?

4. Why do you think Jesus chose to wash his disciples' feet to show them the "full extent" of his love? Why didn't he choose something else?

5. What does this passage teach about leadership and positions of influence? How is this contrary to the world's understanding of power?

6. In verse 17, what's the connection between knowledge and action? Where does blessing come from?

7. Jesus said we should follow his example of service. Practically speaking, what does this mean for you? How can your small group better serve one another? What is one way you can be more of a servant at home? At school? At work?

8. In Jesus' time, servants who washed feet were considered very lowly—after all, who wants to touch someone else's smelly feet, much less wash off all the dirt and sweat on them? Can you think of a modern act of service that would compare to washing feet? How would you feel doing it? Explain.

MINISTRY: SERVING OTHERS IN LOVE

Goal: To recognize and take advantage of opportunities to serve others

It can be difficult to serve on your own. But service can become a lot easier when you're serving with others and working together on a common task.

1. With this in mind, what is one practical way your small group can both serve and work together? Begin a list below. You can always add to the list throughout other small group sessions as you come up with more ideas.

2. Now pick one act of service from your list in which you'd all like to participate. Then set a date and make it happen. Put this lesson into practice.

3. A practical and fun way to develop your serving muscles is to begin a "secret servant" game. Have each person in your group write his or her name on a folded slip of paper, and then secretly pass the names to everyone in the group. The name you receive becomes your "service target" for one week. Your goal is to try to figure out ways you can serve that person in simple yet creative and secretive ways. At the beginning of your next time together, see if you can figure out who served you.

EVANGELISM: SHARING YOUR STORY AND GOD'S STORY

Goal: To consider how the truths from this lesson might be applied to your relationships with unbelievers

A lot of non-Christians perceive that Christians are always doing things with the motive to "capture and convert" them. As a group, try to shatter this stereotype and come up with specific ways you can serve your community without asking for anything in return. For example, there's a youth group in California that does free car washes for the elderly, a youth group in New Hampshire that goes door to door and offers to rake leaves for free, and a youth group in Texas that picks up trash throughout the city on a weekly basis. All of these groups (and hundreds more like them) do this without seeking payment or church attendance; instead, it's their way of serving their community. What do you think about this? What could your group do?

How does this idea connect with evangelism? How can you share God's story without people feeling like a target of "capture and convert"?

WORSHIP: SURRENDERING YOUR LIFE TO HONOR GOD

Goal: To focus on God's presence

1. Finish your group time by confessing and openly admitting that being a servant is difficult and goes against your selfish nature. Share with your group where you'd put yourself on the serving scale below—and share your answer with the group.

1	2	3	4	5	6	7	8	9	10

Serving: it's not for me   *I'm a lot like Jesus*

2. Fill in the blanks below and share them with your group as prayer requests.

   • _____ will be the most difficult act of service for me.
   • This will be difficult because _____ _____.

   Pray for one another about your struggles to serve.

3. One way to end this session is with a foot-washing ceremony. If this is an experience that would benefit your small group, you can read more about this on page 123.

AT HOME THIS WEEK

Option 1: A Weekly Reflection

Take another self-evaluation that reflects five areas of your spiritual life (fellowship, discipleship, ministry, evangelism, worship). See page 73.

Option 2: Daily Bible Readings

Check out the Bible reading plan on page 140.

Option 3: Memory Verses

Memorize another verse from page 145.

Option 4: Journaling

Choose one or more of the following options:

- Write down whatever is on your mind.
- Read your journal entry from last week and write a reflection about it.
- Respond to this question: What would a teenage servant look like in your community?

Option 5: Wrap It Up

Write out your answers to any questions that you didn't answer during your small group time.

LEARN A LITTLE MORE

Goal: To help you better understand the Scripture passage you studied in this session by highlighting key words and other important information

Passover (John 13:1)

During the Passover meal, Jewish people remember how God protected their ancestors from a plague and freed them from Egyptian slavery (see Exodus 12:1-13:10). The plague was God's judgment on the Egyptians for Pharaoh's refusal to free the Israelites. It struck every firstborn child in Egypt, except those in homes where lamb's blood was spread on the doorposts. In an act of love, God passed over the Jewish homes marked with blood. For centuries after, Jews celebrated Passover by eating a sacrificial lamb and other special foods. (They don't sacrifice lambs today!)

Jesus ate his last meal with the disciples on the evening before Passover began. He used this meal to teach some key things about his mission and his desires for their future. With bread and wine, he taught them that his body (bread) and blood (wine) would become the final Passover sacrifice. His death on the cross would free them from slavery to sin and death. And, by washing their feet, he taught them that his life and death were supreme acts of service, and that they should model their lives after his.

Jesus knew (13:3)

Jesus knew his purpose went far beyond the small, even painful acts of service that his Father asked him to do. He served all of humankind by dying on the cross and serves us today with his supernatural love.

Wash his disciples' feet (13:5)

This intimate dinner was kept secret so the disciples could be alone with Jesus; no servant was present to wash their feet when they entered the home. Foot washing was typically the first act upon entering a house (or a tent) after a journey or arrival for a party or feast. In most houses, the guest washed his own feet in water provided by the host. In rich houses, a servant would perform this task. It was considered the lowliest of jobs and could not be required of Jewish slaves. Jesus performed an act of service that only Gentile slaves, wives, or occasionally students would do for their Rabbi—but it was never the other way around! What Jesus did was a radical role reversal. It stunned most of the disciples into silence because they were incredulous that Jesus would perform such a lowly task.

You do not realize now what I am doing (13:7)

The disciples did not yet understand the deep intensity with which Jesus loved them. Washing their feet was nothing compared to what he would do for them in a few hours—endure a slow and violent death on the cross.

A person who has had a bath needs only to wash his feet (13:10)

Peter wasn't ready to give up his argument with Jesus. If his feet needed to be washed, then so did his head and the rest of his body! Jesus graciously explains that Peter did not need that much "cleaning" because Peter had already been bathed. The imagery is that of a guest arriving at a party or feast. Typically they would bathe or wash completely before leaving their home. Once they arrived at the party, only their feet would require washing, as they wore sandals and walked on dusty roads.

FOR DEEPER STUDY ON YOUR OWN

1   Read Philippians 2:1-11 for another picture of Jesus' servant attitude.

Like our society, the ancient world measured people by their social status, not their hearts. If you were a servant, you were nobody. So when the New Testament writers said the Son of God took on "the very nature of a servant" (Philippians 2:7), they meant to shock their readers. It was like saying the world's richest man had decided to work as a field laborer for minimum wage. How is the Philippians passage consistent with what you learned in this session?

2. Why does Jesus use the word *love* to describe the heart of a servant (John 13:34-35; 15:12-13,17; 1 Peter 1:22)?

3. How does 1 Corinthians 13:4-8 help you understand what serving someone actually looks like?

A WEEKLY REFLECTION

Take a minute to reflect on how well you've been doing in the following five areas of your spiritual life this week—a 10 means you were amazing. This reflection can serve as a spiritual gauge to help you consider some very important areas. This is for your personal evaluation and growth; it's NOT a test—no one else needs to see it.

FELLOWSHIP: CONNECTING YOUR HEART TO OTHERS'

How well did I connect with other Christians?

1   2   3   4   5   6   7   8   9   10

DISCIPLESHIP: GROWING TO BE LIKE JESUS

How well did I take steps to grow spiritually and deepen my faith on my own?

1   2   3   4   5   6   7   8   9   10

MINISTRY: SERVING OTHERS IN LOVE

How well did I recognize opportunities to serve others and follow through?

1   2   3   4   5   6   7   8   9   10

EVANGELISM: SHARING YOUR STORY AND GOD'S STORY

How well did I engage in spiritual conversations with non-Christians?

1   2   3   4   5   6   7   8   9   10

WORSHIP: SURRENDERING YOUR LIFE TO HONOR GOD

How well did I focus on God's presence and honor him with my life? Was my relationship with God a primary focus?

1   2   3   4   5   6   7   8   9   10

When you finish, celebrate the areas where you feel good and consider how you can use those strengths to help others in their journey to be more like Jesus. You might also want to take time to identify some potential areas for growth.

JESUS:
THE SAVIOR

⭐ LEADERS, READ PAGE 108.

When Tanisha started going to church with her family, she viewed it as a time and place where she could escape some of her school stress. She was in the middle of a crazy semester of projects, tests, and pressure from college application deadlines. Long nights of studying and tough decisions were wearing her out.

Because several of her close friends were already in college, Tanisha also viewed church as an opportunity to make some new friends. She got involved in the youth ministry and quickly joined a small group. Eventually she began to read her Bible and pray—something she thought she would never do. Up until now, she'd always thought God was a nice idea for others; she didn't really need God because her life was good.

As she got to know some girls in her small group, she shared her anxieties concerning school and college. She felt safe to talk about how lonely she felt during her decision-making process. She was scared to make the wrong choices and face the consequences of messing up the rest of her life. Tanisha felt good talking about her fears with peers.

During one small group session, the topic turned to sin. They read what the Bible taught regarding sin and then began to discuss their own sins—both "big" sins that affected others as well as "small" sins that affected only the sinner. It was an interesting conversation and a unique way to measure sin. In that moment of discussion, Tanisha felt strongly that God cared deeply about both the big and small stuff in her life. This was a new concept to her. Later that night it hit her that the stress from trying to control her life might be a small sin. The more she thought about it, the more she realized that her stress was the result of hanging on to things so tightly.

She quietly asked God to save her from her stress. But in the middle of her prayer, she realized she needed God to save her from all her sins…small and big. It was the first time she admitted her need for a savior.

In this session you will explore why and how Jesus is not just the Savior of the world but also your Savior.

♥ FELLOWSHIP: CONNECTING YOUR HEART TO OTHERS'

Goal: To share about your life and listen attentively to others, caring about what they share

1. Now that you've been in this small group for several weeks, think about the group and your experience as part of it. Which answer best describes how you're feeling? Explain your answer with the group.

    a. It's been really good.
    b. It's better than I thought it was going to be.
    c. It's been good, but I expected something different.
    d. I'd rate it average…at best.
    e. I'd rather watch re-runs at home.
    f. What group?
    g. Other:

DISCIPLESHIP: GROWING TO BE LIKE JESUS

Goal: To explore God's Word, gain biblical knowledge, and make personal applications

In our previous four sessions, we looked at many aspects of Jesus and his ministry. Jesus was a great teacher who revealed the principles and mysteries of God (Session 1). Jesus came to heal the sick (Session 2) and to be a loving shepherd for people (Session 3). Jesus came to serve humanity in the way we needed it most (Session 4).

Ultimately, Jesus came to be the Savior of the world. He paid the price for our sins by dying on the cross so we can enjoy a very real relationship with God.

A Dramatic Narration

It's not unusual for a Christian to say something powerful without fully realizing the power behind the statement—something like "Jesus died for my sins."

It's a worthwhile experience to do something different from what you normally do in your small group and allow the amazing event of Jesus' death affect your heart in a way that you may not have experienced before. For the next several minutes, read the account of Jesus' death aloud—like a play. Have different people read the following roles:

- Narrator (N)
- Jesus (J)
- Pilate, the Roman governor (P)
- Voice of various individuals (V)
- The entire group should read the lines of the Crowd (C) so everyone can experience what it might have been like to participate in the rejection and death of Jesus—the crowd lines are **bold**.

N: When he had finished praying, Jesus left with his disciples and crossed the Kidron Valley. On the other side of the valley was an olive grove that was a familiar place to Jesus and his disciples. Now Judas, who betrayed him, knew the place and came to the grove, guiding a group of soldiers, officials, and Pharisees. They were carrying torches, lanterns, and weapons. Jesus, knowing all that was going to happen to him, went out and asked them,

J: Who is it you want?

C: **Jesus of Nazareth.**

J: I am he.

N: Judas, the traitor, was standing there with them. When Jesus said, "I am he," everyone drew back and fell to the ground. Again he asked them,

J: Who is it you want?

C: **Jesus of Nazareth.**

J: I told you that I am he. If you are looking for me, then let these men go.

N: This happened so that the words he had spoken would be fulfilled: "I have not lost one of those you gave me." Then Simon Peter, who had a sword, drew it and struck the high priest's servant, cutting off his right ear. Jesus commanded Peter,

J: Put your sword away! Shall I not drink the cup the Father has given me?

N: Then the soldiers arrested Jesus. They bound him and brought him first to the high priest. This high priest, Caiaphas, was the one who had advised the Jews that it would be good if one man died for the people. The high priest questioned Jesus about his disciples and his teaching.

J: I have spoken openly to the world. I always taught in synagogues or at the temple, where all the Jews come together. I said nothing in secret. Why question me? Ask those who heard me. Surely they know what I said.

N: When Jesus said this, one of the officials nearby struck him in the face.

V: Is this the way you answer the high priest?

J: If I said something wrong, testify as to what is wrong. But if I spoke the truth, why did you strike me?

N: Then the Jews led Jesus from Caiaphas to the palace of the Roman governor. By now it was early morning, and to avoid ceremonial uncleanness the Jews did not enter the palace; they wanted to be able to eat the Passover. So Pilate came out to them and asked,

P: What charges are you bringing against this man?

C: **If he were not a criminal, we would not have handed him over to you.**

P: Take him yourselves and judge him by your own law.

C: **But we have no right to execute anyone.**

N: This happened so that the words Jesus had spoken indicating the kind of death he was going to die would be fulfilled. Pilate then went back inside the palace, summoned Jesus and asked him,

P: Are you the king of the Jews?

J: Is that your own idea, or did others talk to you about me?

P: Am I a Jew? It was your people and your chief priests who handed you over to me. What is it you have done?

J: My kingdom is not of this world. If it were, my servants would fight to prevent my arrest by the Jews. But now my kingdom is from another place.

P: You are a king, then!

J: You are right in saying I am a king. In fact, for this reason I was born, and for this I came into the world, to testify to the truth. Everyone on the side of truth listens to me.

P: What is truth?

N: Pilate asked. With this he went out again to the Jews and said,

P: I find no basis for a charge against him. But it is your custom for me to release to you one prisoner at the time of the Passover. Do you want me to release "the king of the Jews"?

N: They shouted back,

C: **No, not him! Give us Barabbas!**

N: Now Barabbas had taken part in a rebellion. Then Pilate took Jesus and had him flogged. The soldiers twisted together a crown of thorns and put it on his head. They clothed him in a purple robe and went up to him again and again, saying,

C: **Hail, king of the Jews!**

N: And they struck him in the face. Once more Pilate came out and said to the Jews,

P: Look, I am bringing him out to you to let you know that I find no basis for a charge against him.

N: When Jesus came out wearing the crown of thorns and the purple robe, Pilate said to them,

P: Here is the man!

N: As soon as the chief priests and their officials saw him, they shouted,

C: **Crucify! Crucify!**

N: But Pilate answered,

P: You take him and crucify him. As for me, I find no basis for a charge against him.

C: We have a law, and according to that law he must die, because he claimed to be the Son of God.

N: When Pilate heard this, he was even more afraid, and he went back inside the palace.

P: Where do you come from?

N: he asked Jesus, but Jesus gave him no answer.

P: Do you refuse to speak to me? Don't you realize I have power either to free you or to crucify you?

N: Jesus answered,

J: You would have no power over me if it were not given to you from above. Therefore the one who handed me over to you is guilty of a greater sin.

N: From then on, Pilate tried to set Jesus free, but the Jews kept shouting,

C: If you let this man go, you are no friend of Caesar. Anyone who claims to be a king opposes Caesar.

N: When Pilate heard this, he brought Jesus out and sat down on the judge's seat at a place known as the Stone Pavement (which in Aramaic is Gabbatha). It was the day of preparation of Passover Week, about the sixth hour.

P: Here is your king,

N: Pilate said to the Jews. But they shouted,

C: Take him away! Take him away! Crucify him!

P: Shall I crucify your king?

C: We have no king but Caesar.

N: Finally Pilate handed him over to them to be crucified. So the soldiers took charge of Jesus. Carrying his own cross, he went out to the place of the Skull. Here they crucified him, and with him two others—one on each side and Jesus in the middle.

When the soldiers crucified Jesus, they took his clothes, dividing them into four shares, one for each of them, with the undergarment remaining.

V: Let's not tear it. Let's decide by lot who will get it.

N: This happened that the Scripture might be fulfilled which said, "They divided my garments among them and cast lots for my clothing."

N: Near the cross of Jesus stood his mother, his mother's sister, Mary the wife of Clopas, and Mary Magdalene. When Jesus saw his mother there, and the disciple whom he loved standing nearby, he said to his mother,

J: Dear woman, here is your son,

N: and to the disciple,

J: Here is your mother.

N: From that time on, this disciple took her into his home. Later, knowing that all was now completed, and so that the Scripture would be fulfilled, Jesus said,

J: I am thirsty.

N: A jar of wine vinegar was there, so they soaked a sponge in it, put the sponge on a stalk of the hyssop plant, and lifted it to Jesus' lips. When he had received the drink, Jesus said,

J: It is finished.

N: With that, he bowed his head and gave up his spirit.

Now it was the day of preparation, and the next day was to be a special Sabbath. Because the Jews did not want the bodies left on the crosses during the Sabbath, they asked Pilate to have the legs broken and the bodies taken down. The soldiers therefore came and broke the legs of the first man who had been crucified with Jesus, and then those of the other. But when they came to Jesus and found that he was already dead, they did not break his legs. Instead, one of the soldiers pierced Jesus' side with a spear, bringing a sudden flow of blood and water. The man who saw it has given testimony, and his testimony is true. He knows that he tells the truth, and he testifies so that you also may believe.

(The actual passages from the above reading come from John 18:1-14, 19-23, 28-40; 19:1-35. If you would like to read these passages and you don't have a Bible, you can find the passages on pages 116-121.)

1. As you read this event, what was most significant to you? What words or phrases stood out?

2. What challenges you most in this event?

3. Why did Jesus stop Peter from trying to prevent his arrest (18:10-11)? Wouldn't things have turned out better if Jesus could live longer to heal and teach more people?

4. Jesus said he came into the world "to testify to the truth" (18:37). To what truth did he testify? Why did Pilate ask, "What is truth?" when Jesus had just told him?

5. What did Jesus understand about power that Pilate didn't (19:10-11)?

6. Go back over the words of the crowd. (For example, "Crucify him!" and "We have no king but Caesar.") How do these reflect today's common, human attitudes toward God?

7. *King* is repeated often in this passage. The events hinge on whether and how Jesus is a king. What do you think Pilate's idea of a king is? What kind of king is Jesus?

8. The Gospel of John doesn't give many details about the violence and agony Jesus endured. Why do you suppose it's not in there?

9. The last thing Jesus said was, "It is finished." What does this mean for you personally? What is Jesus talking about, and why does it matter for you? What happens in your own life when you forget or ignore this truth?

EVANGELISM: SHARING YOUR STORY AND GOD'S STORY

Goal: To consider how the truths from this lesson might be applied to your relationships with unbelievers

It's good news that we have a savior in Jesus! In the Bible, "good news" refers to the fact that we can have a relationship with God because of what Jesus did on the cross.

1. Why do you—not the person next to you, but *you*— need a savior?

2. Based on what you know about your non-Christian friends, how would they respond to the idea that they need a savior to be right with God?

3. What are some hurdles that make it difficult for your non-Christian friends to connect with God as their Savior?

MINISTRY: SERVING OTHERS IN LOVE

Goal: To recognize and take advantage of opportunities to serve others

People often open up to the idea of needing a savior after they've made deep, relational connections with others who have asked Jesus to be their Savior and have been following his ways.

What are five practical steps you can take to make these relational connections or friendships? (Don't think of these steps in terms of evangelism. Instead, how can you serve and care for people in such a way that they'll know you love them and want to know more about the source of your love?)

☗ WORSHIP: SURRENDERING YOUR LIFE TO HONOR GOD

Goal: To focus on God's presence

The event that moved Jesus from being just another religious leader to being the Savior of the world was his death on the cross. It wasn't an ordinary death; it was a death that served as payment for our sins. A traditional way that Christians celebrate what Jesus did on the cross is by participating in communion, or the Lord's Supper.

How does your church celebrate communion? Consider planning a time to share communion together. Ask your pastor/leader for guidance, or take a look at www.lifetogether. com for a free download of instructions for sharing communion in a small group.

Before you pray together...

Someone in your group may not have made an authentic connection with Jesus as Savior. This would be a good time to ask questions or discuss what this means without any pressure. After some discussion, ask if anybody wants to begin a connection with Jesus. If so, here's a prayer you might consider praying as a way to begin this connection. You could pray now, later on your own, or with a friend.

Jesus, I want you to be part of my life as my Teacher, Healer, Shepherd, Servant, and especially Savior. I want to follow your ways and live how you want me to live. Please forgive me for trying to live my life without you. Help me to better understand your love for me and to know the good purposes you have for my life. Please help me surround myself with friends who can help me know you better. Amen.

If you already have a connection and a relationship with God through Jesus, take a minute to thank him for all he's done for you.

AT HOME THIS WEEK

Option 1: A Weekly Reflection

Take another self-evaluation that reflects five areas of your spiritual life (fellowship, discipleship, ministry, evangelism, worship). See page 92.

Option 2: Daily Bible Readings

Check out the Bible reading plan on page 140.

Option 3: Memory Verses

Memorize another verse from page 145.

Option 4: Journaling

Choose one or more of the following options:

- Write down whatever is on your mind.
- Read your journal entry from last week and write a reflection about it.
- Respond to this question: Is thinking about Jesus as Savior something you do regularly, or is it easy to forget or overlook? What happens in your life when you lose focus of Jesus as Savior?

Option 5: Wrap It Up

Write out your answers to any questions that you didn't answer during your small group time.

LEARN A LITTLE MORE

Goal: To help you better understand the Scripture passage you studied in this session by highlighting key words and other important information

I am he (John 18:5,6,8)

The language in this phrase is unusual. When Jesus answered in this way, he was saying he was God. (God also used this language in Exodus 3:14.) It's not surprising that the Jewish and Roman guards fell to the ground in terror when they heard a human being use these words.

Caiaphas (18:28)

The Romans officially outlawed the Jewish high priest from carrying out death sentences. But the Jewish authorities didn't want Jesus to become a martyr (dying for his beliefs) and gain even more fame—like John the Baptist. They wanted the Roman governor to execute him as a political criminal.

The Roman governor (18:28)

The Jews had long accused Pontius Pilate of murder, robbery, and other crimes. They rioted when his soldiers paraded through the streets of Jerusalem with an image of the emperor; Jews regarded this as an idol. Pilate's subjects hated him, and Rome would discipline him if there were another uprising in

Jerusalem (either in favor of or in opposition to a supposed Messiah). Pilate couldn't afford to lose the shaky support of the Jewish authorities or the Roman government.

King of the Jews (18:33)

From the Roman point of view, this was a political title. The Messiah/Anointed One/King of the Jews was expected to lead an armed rebellion that would eject the Romans from Israel. Because neither Pilate nor the Jewish authorities understood what the King and his kingdom were really about, Jesus couldn't answer Pilate's question with a simple yes or no.

Flogged (19:1)

A brutal whipping with metal-tipped leather straps.

Crucify (19:6)

Crucifixion was the most feared form of execution the Romans had devised, and they used it for criminals they especially wanted to disgrace. The victim took hours to die while the position of his body forced him to struggle for every breath. Deuteronomy 21:23 declares that "anyone who is hung on a tree is under God's curse," and the Jewish authorities wanted their people to believe that God had cursed Jesus (see also Galatians 3:13).

Disciple whom Jesus loved (19:26)

This disciple was John. Jesus sent his mother to live with him, possibly because her own family was distancing itself from a woman who believed her condemned son was the Messiah.

"It is finished" (19:30)

A single word spoken in Greek, *Tetelestai!* It is a shout of triumph: "It is accomplished!" Archaeologists have found this statement inscribed on pottery from the first century, signifying, "Paid in full." Jesus deliberately took our sin upon himself. In his final moments, he declared that he had paid the full price of our debt and accomplished his mission on earth.

Drink the cup (18:11)

Hours earlier, in the garden where Jesus prayed, twice he pleaded with God:

> "My Father, if it is possible, may this cup be taken from me. Yet not as I will, but as you will" (Matthew 26:39). This cup was God's wrath poured on Jesus as judgment for the sins of the world. Jesus died a real death, but the greater suffering came from being separated (forsaken) by God as he judged the sin that Jesus took upon himself. (See Psalm 22:1, Matthew 27:46, 2 Corinthians 5:21, and Hebrews 9:27-28.)

We have no right to execute anyone (18:31)

The Jews were an occupied nation, and many of their rights had been taken away by the Roman Empire. The Jewish authorities lacked the power to sentence any criminal to death.

The kind of death he was going to die would be fulfilled (18:32)

Crucifixion wasn't practiced among the Jews, although it was common in the Roman Empire. If Jesus had faced a Jewish death sentence, he would have been killed with stones.

He claimed to be the Son of God (19:7)

The most common misconception of Jesus is that he was a "good teacher" who encouraged "moral living." While true, it's also important to note that Jesus' critics were well aware of his claim to be God. In *Mere Christianity*, C. S. Lewis cleverly sums up Jesus' teaching about him being God. Lewis writes that Jesus was (a) who he claimed to be—Lord, (b) a liar, or (c) a lunatic. He definitely wasn't merely a good, moral teacher.

The one who handed me over to you is guilty of a greater sin (19:11)

It is difficult to know exactly whom Jesus was referring to, since so many people betrayed Jesus: the Jewish people, the priests, Caiaphas, Satan, Judas. John's Gospel seems to high-light the betrayal of Caiaphas (see John 11:49-50, 18:13-14), but this isn't clear. What *is* clear is that Pilate had an inflated view of his importance, and while he certainly played a part in Jesus' death, another was even more responsible.

Cast lots (19:24)

Random selection, like rolling dice.

Day of preparation of Passover Week (19:14)

Literally, "Friday of the Passover week." The preparation was for the Sabbath, which came on Saturday.

FOR DEEPER STUDY ON YOUR OWN

1. Read Matthew 26:26-29 to see how Jesus prepared his disciples for his death on the cross. What did he do?

2. Jesus went to the cross on purpose, to be executed in place of the guilty—us. How does Jesus' act affect the way God views and treats you if you have placed your faith in Jesus? Read Romans 5:1-11. How does this truth make you want to respond to God? How does it make you want to respond to others?

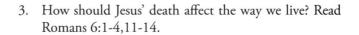

3. How should Jesus' death affect the way we live? Read Romans 6:1-4,11-14.

4. To understand more of what Jesus' death accomplished, see Leviticus 16:1-28, Romans 3:9-26, and Hebrews 9:11-26. What do you learn from these verses?

A WEEKLY REFLECTION

Take a minute to reflect on how well you've been doing in the following five areas of your spiritual life this week—a 10 means you were amazing. This reflection can serve as a spiritual gauge to help you consider some very important areas. This is for your personal evaluation and growth; it's NOT a test—no one else needs to see it.

FELLOWSHIP: CONNECTING YOUR HEART TO OTHERS'
How well did I connect with other Christians?

1   2   3   4   5   6   7   8   9   10

DISCIPLESHIP: GROWING TO BE LIKE JESUS
How well did I take steps to grow spiritually and deepen my faith on my own?

1   2   3   4   5   6   7   8   9   10

MINISTRY: SERVING OTHERS IN LOVE

How well did I recognize opportunities to serve others and follow through?

1   2   3   4   5   6   7   8   9   10

EVANGELISM: SHARING YOUR STORY AND GOD'S STORY

How well did I engage in spiritual conversations with non-Christians?

1   2   3   4   5   6   7   8   9   10

WORSHIP: SURRENDERING YOUR LIFE TO HONOR GOD

How well did I focus on God's presence and honor him with my life? Was my relationship with God a primary focus?

1   2   3   4   5   6   7   8   9   10

When you finish, celebrate the areas where you feel good and consider how you can use those strengths to help others in their journey to be more like Jesus. You might also want to take time to identify some potential areas for growth.

JESUS: THE RISEN LORD

★ LEADERS, READ PAGE 108.

Tyler was a good guy. He had a genuine heart, and everyone loved him. But he was a little unusual for a teenager because he enjoyed volunteering for different charities: Meals on Wheels, community-wide cleanups, nursing homes—basically anything that involved serving others. What made Tyler even more unusual—to some of his friends, anyway—was that he wasn't a Christian. People assumed he was a Christian because of his others-centered lifestyle.

A few of his Christian buddies often invited Tyler to various ministry projects with their youth groups. Tyler loved serving others (even in the name of Jesus), but he had never made a personal commitment to follow God's way and put his faith in Jesus as his Savior. He knew the basics of Christianity, but he thought he was a good person and didn't need a relationship with Jesus. He'd decided that Jesus was for people who weren't good on their own. Basically, Tyler believed that his good works and generous life had him covered in the spiritual world.

One terrible night, Tyler's older brother was killed in a car accident. It rocked the family and began a season of confusion and loneliness in Tyler. No amount of charity work could make this pain go away. Tyler felt as though he had nothing to hold on to and struggled with the question of why something so bad could happen to such a good person. He searched for answers but couldn't find peace.

Tyler's friend Dave had invited him to church on many occasions. If it was a service project, Tyler went. If it was just youth group, he had no interest. The one time Tyler changed his mind was the night that changed his life forever. He went to church with Dave and heard a message on the resurrection of Jesus. Tyler realized he was powerless to change his life on his own strength and surrendered his entire life to Jesus and the power that raised Jesus from the dead. In the midst of his pain, Jesus met Tyler and began healing him, and slowly Tyler began to trust that God was in control.

In this session you'll discuss the resurrection of Jesus and see how the power that raised him from the dead is available to you in your everyday life.

♥ FELLOWSHIP: CONNECTING YOUR HEART TO OTHERS

Goal: To share about your life and listen attentively to others, caring about what they share

Why are you glad you've been part of this group? Simply finish one of the following sentences:

   a. Because of [name of person] and [what he or she did].
   b. Because I have learned _____.
   c. If I hadn't been here, I wouldn't have _____
      _____.
   d. Life would still be _____.
   e. Other:

DISCIPLESHIP: GROWING TO BE LIKE JESUS

Goal: To explore God's Word, gain biblical knowledge, and make personal applications

As you examine the biblical account of Jesus' resurrection, you'll need to understand that this miracle is the "main event" of the Christian life. The resurrection of Jesus demonstrated (a) the power of God, (b) the truth of Jesus' teaching, and (c) the fulfillment of prophecy.

When Jesus died, the disciples thought their dreams of him being the Messiah died with him. But when they saw him alive again, they began to understand everything he had told them.

The resurrection of Jesus isn't just a happy ending to a cute story. The resurrection is an invitation to a fresh start. The resurrection proved that Jesus was who he said he was. He defeated death, and that changes everything—for humanity, for you, and for eternity!

Read John 20:1-23. **(If you don't have a Bible, the passage is on page 121-122.)**

1. As you read about this event, notice that John gives many specific details about the circumstances related to the empty tomb. Why do you think this is?

2. When Mary Magdalene first found the empty tomb, what made her so sad?

   What did Peter and John (the disciple whom Jesus loved) think happened? Is there a verse in the text that directly answers these questions?

3. Although John arrived at the tomb first, Peter went in first. What does this tell you about Peter's character? (See verses 5-6.) Once John went inside, he saw the same thing Peter did, yet John is the one who immediately believed. What does this tell you about John's character?

4. Once Mary Magdalene realized Jesus had risen from the dead, what did Jesus tell her to do?

5. Why did angels appear to Mary Magdalene and not the disciples? Is there any clear answer from the text?

6. What question does Jesus ask Mary Magdalene—twice? What does this teach us about the resurrection?

7. Why is it important that the bandages (strips of linen, burial cloth, etc.) were left in the tomb? If the disciples had taken the body, do you think they would have left the bandages in disarray or taken the time to fold some of them (verse 7)?

8. What do you think the disciples were thinking in the moments before Jesus appeared to them?

9. In your opinion, why did Jesus show them his hands and his side?

10. Why is it important to you that Jesus rose from the dead?

👣 MINISTRY: SERVING OTHERS IN LOVE

Goal: To recognize and take advantage of opportunities to serve others

Jesus doesn't just offer us eternal life after death. He offers us new life, here and now, and the power to live life to its fullest (John 10:10). We can live each day as followers of Jesus with the same power that was used for the resurrection—resurrection power through the Holy Spirit (John 20:22). Too often Christians minimize the power of the gospel because they don't understand how it can change their lives here on earth.

1. If you really believed that God's power were available to you today, what would you ask him to do with your life? How could your life make the earth a better place?

2. If you're meeting prior to Easter, you might consider a way that your small group can serve your church on or around Easter Sunday. The message of Easter is the message that Jesus is the risen Lord. Remember that your service may help others in your church (and your community) come to know Jesus as Savior.

👄 EVANGELISM: SHARING YOUR STORY AND GOD'S STORY

Goal: To consider how the truths from this lesson might be applied to your relationships with unbelievers

In Session 4, you were challenged to find someone younger whom you could shepherd (page 54). Now that you've been through this entire book, you might consider leading that person through this book, too! With everything you've learned about Jesus, you have a lot to pass on to others.

1. Do you think you could lead someone through this study? Why, or why not?

2. Who would that person be and when could you meet? (Make sure you still have time to commit to this group and the other studies in this series!)

3. Do you have any fears about guiding another person through these sessions? If yes, what are they?

4. Respond to this statement: "If you take a Christian through this book—that's primarily an act of discipleship. If you take a non-Christian through this book— that's probably going to be a more evangelistic time."

5. Why do you think the resurrection of Jesus is the part of the gospel that many non-Christians have the most trouble believing?

🚶 WORSHIP: SURRENDERING YOUR LIFE TO HONOR GOD

Goal: To focus on God's presence

Since this is the last time your group will be together with this particular book as your guide, make sure you take some time to discuss what will happen to your group next. If you want to continue to study the incredible life and teachings of Jesus, there are five more books in this series.

1. Take some time to share if anyone prayed a prayer of commitment similar to the one on page 87. How can you support each other in your decisions to follow Christ?

2. Have everyone in the group take a turn reading the following verse out loud. After everyone is finished, sit in silence for one minute and think about what it means to you right now (that's meditation). Then write a brief paraphrase of the verse in your own words.

   All honor to the God and Father of our Lord Jesus Christ, for it is by his boundless mercy that God has given us the privilege of being born again. Now we live with a wonderful expectation because Jesus Christ rose again from the dead. (1 Peter 1:3)

   In my own words, this verse says…

3. Before you close in prayer together, consider how the resurrection of Jesus affects you today in these ways:

   - Jesus' resurrection demonstrates that he really is the Son of God (Romans 1:4), and that everything he taught was the truth.
   - Jesus' resurrection frees you from the fear of death (1 Corinthians 15:54-58, Hebrews 2:14-15).
   - Jesus' resurrection shows that death has no final hold over you. You have nothing to fear from aging, disease, or failure, either, because none of those is final. You're going to live eternally with God and his people. You don't need to fear the eternal separation from God that awaits those who reject him (Matthew 25:31-46).
   - Jesus' resurrection frees you from spiritual death (Ephesians 2:1-7).

- You can have an intimate connection with God right now.
- Jesus' resurrection gives you the chance to live with his life in you, free from the power of sin that would otherwise enslave you (Romans 6:5-14).
- If you cooperate with Jesus, you have access to the power to reject sin.

4. Which one of these truths most motivates you to surrender your life to God?

AT HOME THIS WEEK

Option 1: A Weekly Reflection

Take another self-evaluation that reflects five areas of your spiritual life (fellowship, discipleship, ministry, evangelism, worship). See page 105.

Option 2: Daily Bible Readings

Check out the Bible reading plan on page 140.

Option 3: Memory Verses

Memorize another verse from page 145.

Option 4: Journaling

Choose one or more of the following options:

- Write down whatever is on your mind.
- Read your journal entry from last week and write a reflection about it.
- Respond to this question: "Coming face to face with the resurrected Jesus, the disciples were filled with peace and joy" (John 20:19-20). Do these two words describe your life? In what areas are you lacking joy and peace?

Option 5: Wrap It Up

Write out your answers to any questions that you didn't answer during your small group time.

LEARN A LITTLE MORE

Goal: To help you better understand the Scripture passage you studied in this session by highlighting key words and other important information

First day of the week (John 20:1)

According to the Jewish calendar, Sunday is the first day of the week; Saturday is the last day of the week—because it was the seventh day of creation. It is also the Jewish Sabbath.

The tomb (20:1)

During the time of Jesus, most burial tombs in Israel were actually caves. These caves often had low, narrow openings that were sealed shut by a stone. Inside the cave could be multiple burial chambers. The body rested on a bench or in a dug-out niche. Tombs were often decorated because families owned them for generations. They would be used over and over again because once the body had decayed and only bones were left, the bones were transferred to a second burial place called an ossuary—a stone chest with a lid.

Strips of linen... burial cloth (20:5-7)

It was a Jewish burial custom to wrap a dead body in linen strips dipped and hardened together with ointments. Joseph and Nicodemus used about 75 pounds of the sticky mixture to wrap Jesus (19:39-40). This type of royal burial cost a lot of money—and made it virtually impossible for thieves to unglue the wrappings from the body. One of the ointments, myrrh, "glues linen to the body not less firmly than lead." [2] That's why the sight of the wrappings without the body was so noteworthy.

They still did not understand from Scripture that Jesus had to rise from the dead (20:9)

Though Jesus told his disciples about his death and resurrection (Matthew 16:21), they couldn't fully grasp the concept or understand its significance. But after his resurrection, they were able to understand many more of the statements that Jesus had made while he was teaching them.

If you forgive anyone his sins, they are forgiven (20:23)

In Matthew 16:19, Jesus gave Peter and the other disciples the keys to God's kingdom. He also gave them the authority (Matthew 28:18) to preach the gospel and lead others to God's kingdom. Here Jesus reminds them of their duty once again, this time under the guiding power of the Holy Spirit (John 20:22, Acts 1:8).

FOR DEEPER STUDY ON YOUR OWN

1. Check out this account from the other Gospel writers: Matthew 28:1-8, Mark 16:1-8, and Luke 24:1-10.

2. Look at Scriptures below that predict Jesus' resurrection:

   - Psalm 16:10 says, "You will not abandon me to the grave, nor will you let your Holy One see decay." (Compare this to Acts 2:25-31.)
   - Isaiah 53:11 says, "After the suffering of his soul, he will see the light of life and be satisfied."

[2] Leon Morris, *The Gospel According to John* (Grand Rapids, Mich.: Eerdmans, 1971), p. 833, note 16. Morris cites the early church father John Chrysostom for this information.

A WEEKLY REFLECTION

Take a minute to reflect on how well you've been doing in the following five areas of your spiritual life this week—a 10 means you were amazing. This reflection can serve as a spiritual gauge to help you consider some very important areas. This is for your personal evaluation and growth; it's NOT a test—no one else needs to see it.

FELLOWSHIP: CONNECTING YOUR HEART TO OTHERS'

How well did I connect with other Christians?

1   2   3   4   5   6   7   8   9   10

DISCIPLESHIP: GROWING TO BE LIKE JESUS

How well did I take steps to grow spiritually and deepen my faith on my own?

1   2   3   4   5   6   7   8   9   10

MINISTRY: SERVING OTHERS IN LOVE

How well did I recognize opportunities to serve others and follow through?

1   2   3   4   5   6   7   8   9   10

EVANGELISM: SHARING YOUR STORY AND GOD'S STORY

How well did I engage in spiritual conversations with non-Christians?

1   2   3   4   5   6   7   8   9   10

WORSHIP: SURRENDERING YOUR LIFE TO HONOR GOD

How well did I focus on God's presence and honor him with my life? Was my relationship with God a primary focus?

1   2   3   4   5   6   7   8   9   10

When you finish, celebrate the areas where you feel good and consider how you can use those strengths to help others in their journey to be more like Jesus. You might also want to take time to identify some potential areas for growth.

APPENDICES

SMALL GROUP LEADER CHECKLIST

☐ Read through "For Small Group Leaders: How to Best Use This Material" (see pages 109-112).

This is very important—familiarizing yourself with it will help you understand content and how to best manage your time.

☐ Read through all the questions in the session you'll be leading

The questions are a guide for you to help students grow spiritually. Think through which questions are best for your group. Remember, no curriculum author knows your students better than you do! Just a small amount of preparation on your part will help you manage the time you'll have with your group. Based on the amount of time you'll have in your small group, circle the questions you will discuss as a group. Decide what (if anything) you will assign at the end of the session (things like homework, snacks, group projects, and so on).

☐ Remember that the questions in this book don't always have obvious, neat, tidy answers.

Some are purposely written to cause good discussion without a specific "right" answer. Often questions (and answers) will lead to more questions.

☐ Make sure you have enough books for your students and a few extra in case your students invite friends.

(Note: It's vital for your group to decide during the first session whether you can invite friends to join your group. If not, encourage your group to think of friends they can invite if you go through the next EXPERIENCING CHRIST TOGETHER book in this series.)

☐ Read the material included in this appendix.

It's filled with information that will benefit your group and your student ministry. This appendix alone is a great reference for students—familiarize yourself with the tools here so you can offer them to students.

☐ Submit your leadership and your group to God.

Ask God to provide you with insight into how to lead your group, patience to do so, and courage to speak the truth in love when needed.

FOR SMALL GROUP LEADERS: HOW TO BEST USE THIS MATERIAL

This book was written more as a guidebook than a workbook. In most workbooks, you're supposed to answer every question and fill in all the blanks. In this book, there are lots of questions and plenty of blank space. Explain to your students that this isn't a school workbook—they're not graded on how much they've written.

The number-one rule for this curriculum is that there are no rules apart from the ones you decide to use. Every small group is unique and will figure out its own style and system. (The exception is when the lead youth worker establishes a guideline for all the groups to follow. In that case, respect your leader's guidelines.)

If you need a guide to get you started until you navigate your own way, here's one way you might adapt the material for a 60-minute session.

Introduction (4 minutes)

Begin each session with one student reading the Small Group Covenant (see page 18). This becomes a constant reminder of why you'll be doing what you're doing. Then have another student read the opening paragraphs of the session you'll be discussing. Allow different students to take turns reading these two opening pieces.

Connecting (10 minutes)

This section can take 45 minutes if you're not careful! You'll need to stay on task to keep this segment short—consider giving students a specific amount of time and holding them to it. It's always better to leave students wanting more time for discussion than to leave them bored.

Growing (25 minutes)

Read God's Word and work through the questions you think will be best for your group. This section definitely has more questions than you'll be able to discuss in the allotted time. Before the small group begins, take some time to read through the questions and choose the best ones for your group. You may also want to add questions of your own. If someone forgets a Bible, we've provided the Scripture passages for each session in the appendix.

If your small group is biblically mature, this section won't be too difficult. However, if your group struggles with these questions, make sure you sift through them and focus on the few questions that will help drive the message home. Also, you might want to encourage your group to answer the remaining questions on their own.

Serving and Sharing (10 minutes)

If you're pressed for time, you may choose to skip one of these two sections. If you do need to skip one due to time constraints, group members can finish the section on their own during the week. Don't feel guilty about passing over a section. **One of the strengths of this material is the built-in, intentional repetition in every session. You will have other opportunities to discuss that biblical purpose.** (Again, that's the main reason for spending a few minutes before your group meets to read through all the questions and pick the best ones for your group.)

Surrendering (10 minutes)

We always want to end the lesson with a focus on God and a specific time of prayer. You'll have several options but feel free to default to your group's comfort level.

Closing Challenge (1 minute)

Encourage students to pick one option each from the "At Home This Week" section to complete on their own. The more students initiate and develop the habit of spending time with God, the healthier their spiritual journeys will be. We've found that students have plenty of unanswered questions that they will consider on their own time. **Keep in mind that the main goal of this book is building spiritual growth in community—not to get your students to answer every question correctly.** Remember that this is your small group, your time, and the questions will always be there. Use them, ignore them, or assign them for personal study during the week—but don't feel pressure to follow this curriculum exactly or "grade" your group's biblical knowledge.

Finally, remember that questions are a great way to get students connected to one another and God's Word. You don't have to have all the answers.

Suggestions for Existing Small Groups

If your small group has been meeting for a while, and you've already established comfortable relationships, you can jump right into the material. But make sure you take the following actions, even if you're a well-established group:

- Read through the "Small Group Covenant" on page 18 and make additions or adjustments as necessary.

- Read the "Prayer Request Guidelines" together (page 158). You can maximize the group's time by following them.

- Before each meeting, consider whether you'll assign material to be completed (or at least thought through) before your next meeting.

- Familiarize yourself with all the "At Home This Week" options at the end of each session. They are explained in detail near the end of Session 1 (page 27), and then briefly summarized at the end of the other five sessions.

Although handling business like this can seem cumbersome or unnecessary to an existing group, these foundational steps can save you from headaches later on because you took the time to create an environment conducive to establishing deep relationships.

Suggestions for New Small Groups

If your group is meeting together for the first time, jumping right into the first session may not be your best option. You may want to meet as a group before you begin going through the book so you can get to know each other better. To prepare for the first gathering, read and follow the "Suggestions for Existing Groups" mentioned previously.

Spend some time getting to know each other with icebreaker questions. Several are listed here. Pick one or two that will work best for your group or use your own. The goal is to break ground so you can plant the seeds of healthy relationships.

1. What's your name, school, grade, and favorite class in school? (Picking your least favorite class is too easy.)

2. Tell the group a brief (basic) history of your family. What's your family life like? How many brothers and sisters do you have? Which family members are you closest to?

3. What's one thing about yourself that you really like?

4. Everyone has little personality quirks—traits that make each one of us unique. What are yours?

5. Why did you choose to be a part of this small group?

6. What do you hope to get out of this small group? How do you expect it to help you?

7. What do you think it will take to make our small group work well?

Need some teaching help?

Companion DVDs are available for each EXPERIENCING CHRIST TOGETHER book. These DVDs contain teaching segments you can use to supplement each session. Play them before your discussion begins or just prior to the "Grow" section in each session. The DVDs aren't required, but they are a great complement and supplement to the small group material. These are available from www.youthspecialties.com.

SCRIPTURE PASSAGES

Session 1

Mark 1:14-28

[14] After John was put in prison, Jesus went into Galilee, proclaiming the good news of God. [15] "The time has come," he said. "The kingdom of God is near. Repent and believe the good news!" [16] As Jesus walked beside the Sea of Galilee, he saw Simon and his brother Andrew casting a net into the lake, for they were fishermen. [17] "Come, follow me," Jesus said, "and I will make you fishers of men." [18] At once they left their nets and followed him. [19] When he had gone a little farther, he saw James son of Zebedee and his brother John in a boat, preparing their nets. [20] Without delay he called them, and they left their father Zebedee in the boat with the hired men and followed him. [21] They went to Capernaum, and when the Sabbath came, Jesus went into the synagogue and began to teach. [22] The people were amazed at his teaching, because he taught them as one who had authority, not as the teachers of the law.

[23] Just then a man in their synagogue who was possessed by an evil spirit cried out, [24] "What do you want with us, Jesus of Nazareth? Have you come to destroy us? I know who you are—the Holy One of God!" [25] "Be quiet!" said Jesus sternly. "Come out of him!" [26] The evil spirit shook the man violently and came out of him with a shriek. [27] The people were all so amazed that they asked each other, "What is this? A new teaching—and with authority! He even gives orders to evil spirits and they obey him." [28] News about him spread quickly over the whole region of Galilee.

Session 2

Mark 1:40-45

[40] A man with leprosy came to him and begged him on his knees, "If you are willing, you can make me clean." [41] Filled with compassion, Jesus reached out his hand and touched the man. "I am willing," he said. "Be clean!" [42] Immediately the leprosy left him and he was cured. [43] Jesus sent him away at once with a strong warning: [44] "See that you don't tell this to anyone. But go, show yourself to the priest and offer the sacrifices that Moses commanded for your cleansing, as a testimony to them." [45] Instead he went out and began to talk freely, spreading the news. As a result, Jesus could no longer enter a town openly but stayed outside in lonely places. Yet the people still came to him from everywhere.

Mark 2:1-12

[1] A few days later, when Jesus again entered Capernaum, the people heard that he had come home. [2] So many gathered that there was no room left, not even outside the door, and he preached the word to them. [3] Some men came, bringing to him a paralytic, carried by four of them. [4] Since they could not get him to Jesus because of the crowd, they made an opening in the roof above Jesus and, after digging through it, lowered the mat the paralyzed man was lying on. [5] When Jesus saw their faith, he said to the paralytic, "Son, your sins are forgiven." [6] Now some teachers of the law were sitting there, thinking to themselves, [7] "Why does this fellow talk like that? He's blaspheming! Who can forgive sins but God alone?" [8] Immediately Jesus knew in his spirit that this was what they were thinking in their hearts, and he said to them, "Why are you thinking these things? [9] Which is easier: to say to the paralytic, 'Your sins are forgiven,' or to say, 'Get up, take your mat and walk'? [10] But that you may know that the Son of Man has authority on earth to forgive sins...." He said to the paralytic, [11] "I tell you, get up, take your mat and go home." [12] He got up, took his mat and walked out in full view of them all. This amazed everyone and they praised God, saying, "We have never seen anything like this!"

Session 3

John 10:1-5

[1] "I tell you the truth, the man who does not enter the sheep pen by the gate, but climbs in by some other way, is a thief and a robber. [2] The man who enters by the gate is the shepherd of his sheep. [3] The watchman opens the gate for him, and the sheep listen to his voice. He calls his own sheep by name and leads them out. [4] When he has brought out all his own, he goes on ahead of them, and his sheep follow him because they know his voice. [5] But they will never follow a stranger; in fact, they will run away from him because they do not recognize a stranger's voice."

John 10:6-10

[6] Jesus used this figure of speech, but they did not understand what he was telling them. [7] Therefore Jesus said again, "I tell you the truth, I am the gate for the sheep. [8] All who ever came before me were thieves and robbers, but the sheep did not listen to them. [9] I am the gate; whoever enters through me will be saved. He will come in and go out, and find pasture. [10] The thief comes only to steal and kill and destroy; I have come that they may have life, and have it to the full.

John 10:11-18

[11] "I am the good shepherd. The good shepherd lays down his life for the sheep. [12] The hired hand is not the shepherd who owns the sheep. So when he sees the wolf coming, he abandons the sheep and runs away. Then the wolf attacks the flock and scatters it. [13] The man runs away because he is a hired hand and cares nothing for the sheep. [14] "I am the good shepherd; I know my sheep and my sheep know me [15] just as the Father knows me and I know the Father and I lay down my life for the sheep. [16] I have other sheep that are not of this sheep pen. I must bring them also. They too will listen to my voice, and there shall be one flock and one shepherd. [17] The reason my Father loves me is that I lay down my life only to take it up again. [18] No one takes it from me, but I lay it down of my own accord. I have authority to lay it down and authority to take it up again. This command I received from my Father."

Psalm 23

[1] The Lord is my shepherd, I shall not be in want.

[2] He makes me lie down in green pastures,

he leads me beside quiet waters,

[3] he restores my soul.

He guides me in paths of righteousness

for his name's sake.

[4] Even though I walk

through the valley of the shadow of death,

I will fear no evil,

for you are with me;

your rod and your staff,

they comfort me.

[5] You prepare a table before me

in the presence of my enemies.

You anoint my head with oil;

my cup overflows.

[6] Surely goodness and love will follow me

all the days of my life,

and I will dwell in the house of the Lord

forever.

Session 4

John 13: 1-17

[1] It was just before the Passover Feast. Jesus knew that the time had come for him to leave this world and go to the Father. Having loved his own who were in the world, he now showed them the full extent of his love. [2] The evening meal was being served, and the devil had already prompted Judas Iscariot, son of Simon, to betray Jesus. [3] Jesus knew that the Father had put all things under his power, and that he had come from God and was returning to God; [4] so he got up from the meal, took off his outer clothing, and wrapped a towel around his waist. [5] After that, he poured water into a basin and began to wash his disciples' feet, drying them with the towel that was wrapped around him. [6] He came to Simon Peter, who said to him, "Lord, are you going to wash my feet?" [7] Jesus replied, "You do not realize now what I am doing, but later you will understand." [8] "No," said Peter, "you shall never wash my feet." Jesus answered, "Unless I wash you, you have no part with me." [9] "Then, Lord," Simon Peter replied, "not just my feet but my hands and my head as well!" [10] Jesus answered, "A person who has had a bath needs only to wash his feet; his whole body is clean. And you are clean, though not every one of you." [11] For he knew who was going to betray him, and that was why he said not every one was clean. [12] When he had finished washing their feet, he put on his clothes and returned to his place. "Do you understand what I have done for you?" he asked them. [13] "You call me 'Teacher' and 'Lord,' and rightly so, for that is what I am. [14] Now that I, your Lord and Teacher, have washed your feet, you also should wash one another's feet. [15] I have set you an example that you should do as I have done for you. [16] I tell you the truth, no servant is greater than his master, nor is a messenger greater than the one who sent him. [17] Now that you know these things, you will be blessed if you do them.

Session 5

John 18:1-14

[1] When he had finished praying, Jesus left with his disciples and crossed the Kidron Valley. On the other side there was an olive grove, and he and his disciples went into it.

[2] Now Judas, who betrayed him, knew the place, because Jesus had often met there with his disciples. [3] So Judas came to the grove, guiding a detachment of soldiers and some officials from the chief priests and Pharisees. They were carrying torches, lanterns and weapons.

⁴ Jesus, knowing all that was going to happen to him, went out and asked them, "Who is it you want?"

⁵ "Jesus of Nazareth," they replied.

"I am he," Jesus said. (And Judas the traitor was standing there with them.) ⁶ When Jesus said, "I am he," they drew back and fell to the ground.

⁷ Again he asked them, "Who is it you want?"

And they said, "Jesus of Nazareth."

⁸ "I told you that I am he," Jesus answered. "If you are looking for me, then let these men go." ⁹ This happened so that the words he had spoken would be fulfilled: "I have not lost one of those you gave me."

¹⁰ Then Simon Peter, who had a sword, drew it and struck the high priest's servant, cutting off his right ear. (The servant's name was Malchus.)

¹¹ Jesus commanded Peter, "Put your sword away! Shall I not drink the cup the Father has given me?"

¹² Then the detachment of soldiers with its commander and the Jewish officials arrested Jesus. They bound him ¹³ and brought him first to Annas, who was the father-in-law of Caiaphas, the high priest that year. ¹⁴ Caiaphas was the one who had advised the Jews that it would be good if one man died for the people.

John 18:19-23

¹⁹ Meanwhile, the high priest questioned Jesus about his disciples and his teaching.

²⁰ "I have spoken openly to the world," Jesus replied. "I always taught in synagogues or at the temple, where all the Jews come together. I said nothing in secret. ²¹ Why question me? Ask those who heard me. Surely they know what I said."

²² When Jesus said this, one of the officials nearby struck him in the face. "Is this the way you answer the high priest?" he demanded.

²³ "If I said something wrong," Jesus replied, "testify as to what is wrong. But if I spoke the truth, why did you strike me?"

John 18:28-40

28 Then the Jews led Jesus from Caiaphas to the palace of the Roman governor. By now it was early morning, and to avoid ceremonial uncleanness the Jews did not enter the palace; they wanted to be able to eat the Passover. 29 So Pilate came out to them and asked, "What charges are you bringing against this man?"

30 "If he were not a criminal," they replied, "we would not have handed him over to you."

31 Pilate said, "Take him yourselves and judge him by your own law."

"But we have no right to execute anyone," the Jews objected. 32 This happened so that the words Jesus had spoken indicating the kind of death he was going to die would be fulfilled.

33 Pilate then went back inside the palace, summoned Jesus and asked him, "Are you the king of the Jews?"

34 "Is that your own idea," Jesus asked, "or did others talk to you about me?"

35 "Am I a Jew?" Pilate replied. "It was your people and your chief priests who handed you over to me. What is it you have done?"

36 Jesus said, "My kingdom is not of this world. If it were, my servants would fight to prevent my arrest by the Jews. But now my kingdom is from another place."

37 "You are a king, then!" said Pilate.

Jesus answered, "You are right in saying I am a king. In fact, for this reason I was born, and for this I came into the world, to testify to the truth. Everyone on the side of truth listens to me."

38 "What is truth?" Pilate asked. With this he went out again to the Jews and said, "I find no basis for a charge against him. 39 But it is your custom for me to release to you one prisoner at the time of the Passover. Do you want me to release 'the king of the Jews'?"

40 They shouted back, "No, not him! Give us Barabbas!" Now Barabbas had taken part in a rebellion.

John 19:1-35

[1] Then Pilate took Jesus and had him flogged. [2] The soldiers twisted together a crown of thorns and put it on his head. They clothed him in a purple robe [3] and went up to him again and again, saying, "Hail, king of the Jews!" And they struck him in the face.

[4] Once more Pilate came out and said to the Jews, "Look, I am bringing him out to you to let you know that I find no basis for a charge against him." [5] When Jesus came out wearing the crown of thorns and the purple robe, Pilate said to them, "Here is the man!"

[6] As soon as the chief priests and their officials saw him, they shouted, "Crucify! Crucify!"

But Pilate answered, "You take him and crucify him. As for me, I find no basis for a charge against him."

[7] The Jews insisted, "We have a law, and according to that law he must die, because he claimed to be the Son of God."

[8] When Pilate heard this, he was even more afraid, [9] and he went back inside the palace. "Where do you come from?" he asked Jesus, but Jesus gave him no answer. [10] "Do you refuse to speak to me?" Pilate said. "Don't you realize I have power either to free you or to crucify you?"

[11] Jesus answered, "You would have no power over me if it were not given to you from above. Therefore the one who handed me over to you is guilty of a greater sin."

[12] From then on, Pilate tried to set Jesus free, but the Jews kept shouting, "If you let this man go, you are no friend of Caesar. Anyone who claims to be a king opposes Caesar."

[13] When Pilate heard this, he brought Jesus out and sat down on the judge's seat at a place known as the Stone Pavement (which in Aramaic is Gabbatha). [14] It was the day of preparation of Passover Week, about the sixth hour.

"Here is your king," Pilate said to the Jews.

[15] But they shouted, "Take him away! Take him away! Crucify him!"

"Shall I crucify your king?" Pilate asked.

"We have no king but Caesar," the chief priests answered.

¹⁶ Finally Pilate handed him over to them to be crucified.

So the soldiers took charge of Jesus. ¹⁷ Carrying his own cross, he went out to the place of the Skull (which in Aramaic is called Golgotha). ¹⁸ Here they crucified him, and with him two others—one on each side and Jesus in the middle.

¹⁹ Pilate had a notice prepared and fastened to the cross. It read: JESUS OF NAZARETH, THE KING OF THE JEWS. ²⁰ Many of the Jews read this sign, for the place where Jesus was crucified was near the city, and the sign was written in Aramaic, Latin and Greek. ²¹ The chief priests of the Jews protested to Pilate, "Do not write 'The King of the Jews,' but that this man claimed to be king of the Jews."

²² Pilate answered, "What I have written, I have written."

²³ When the soldiers crucified Jesus, they took his clothes, dividing them into four shares, one for each of them, with the undergarment remaining. This garment was seamless, woven in one piece from top to bottom.

²⁴ "Let's not tear it," they said to one another. "Let's decide by lot who will get it."

This happened that the scripture might be fulfilled which said,

"They divided my garments among them

and cast lots for my clothing."

So this is what the soldiers did.

²⁵ Near the cross of Jesus stood his mother, his mother's sister, Mary the wife of Clopas, and Mary Magdalene. ²⁶ When Jesus saw his mother there, and the disciple whom he loved standing nearby, he said to his mother, "Dear woman, here is your son," ²⁷ and to the disciple, "Here is your mother." From that time on, this disciple took her into his home.

²⁸ Later, knowing that all was now completed, and so that the Scripture would be fulfilled, Jesus said, "I am thirsty." ²⁹ A jar of wine vinegar was there, so they soaked a sponge in it, put the sponge on a stalk of the hyssop plant, and lifted it to Jesus' lips. ³⁰ When he had received the drink, Jesus said, "It is finished." With that, he bowed his head and gave up his spirit.

³¹ Now it was the day of Preparation, and the next day was to be a special Sabbath. Because the Jews did not want the bodies left on the crosses during the Sabbath, they asked Pilate to have the legs broken and the bod-

ies taken down. [32] The soldiers therefore came and broke the legs of the first man who had been crucified with Jesus, and then those of the other. [33] But when they came to Jesus and found that he was already dead, they did not break his legs. [34] Instead, one of the soldiers pierced Jesus' side with a spear, bringing a sudden flow of blood and water. [35] The man who saw it has given testimony, and his testimony is true. He knows that he tells the truth, and he testifies so that you also may believe.

Session 6
John 20:1-23

[1] Early on the first day of the week, while it was still dark, Mary Magdalene went to the tomb and saw that the stone had been removed from the entrance. [2] So she came running to Simon Peter and the other disciple, the one Jesus loved, and said, "They have taken the Lord out of the tomb, and we don't know where they have put him!" [3] So Peter and the other disciple started for the tomb. [4] Both were running, but the other disciple outran Peter and reached the tomb first. [5] He bent over and looked in at the strips of linen lying there but did not go in. [6] Then Simon Peter, who was behind him, arrived and went into the tomb. He saw the strips of linen lying there, [7] as well as the burial cloth that had been around Jesus' head. The cloth was folded up by itself, separate from the linen. [8] Finally the other disciple, who had reached the tomb first, also went inside. He saw and believed. [9] (They still did not understand from Scripture that Jesus had to rise from the dead.) [10] Then the disciples went back to their homes, [11] but Mary stood outside the tomb crying. As she wept, she bent over to look into the tomb [12] and saw two angels in white, seated where Jesus' body had been, one at the head and the other at the foot. [13] They asked her, "Woman, why are you crying?" "They have taken my Lord away," she said, "and I don't know where they have put him." [14] At this, she turned around and saw Jesus standing there, but she did not realize that it was Jesus. [15] "Woman," he said, "why are you crying? Who is it you are looking for?" Thinking he was the gardener, she said, "Sir, if you have carried him away, tell me where you have put him, and I will get him." [16] Jesus said to her, "Mary." She turned toward him and cried out in Aramaic, "Rabboni!" (which means Teacher). [17] Jesus said, "Do not hold on to me, for I have not yet returned to the Father. Go instead to my brothers and tell them, 'I am returning to my Father and your Father, to my God and your God.'" [18] Mary Magdalene went to the disciples with the news: "I have seen the Lord!" And she told

them that he had said these things to her. [19] On the evening of that first day of the week, when the disciples were together, with the doors locked for fear of the Jews, Jesus came and stood among them and said, "Peace be with you!" [20] After he said this, he showed them his hands and side. The disciples were overjoyed when they saw the Lord. [21] Again Jesus said, "Peace be with you! As the Father has sent me, I am sending you." [22] And with that he breathed on them and said, "Receive the Holy Spirit. [23] If you forgive anyone his sins, they are forgiven; if you do not forgive them, they are not forgiven."

FOOT-WASHING EXPERIENCE

If your group is ready for this experience, this is an alternative to the Worship section in Session 4. Not all groups are ready for this exercise—don't worry if it's not right for your group. Read the following and decide what's best. Also, decide if you will wash a few feet or all the feet in your group.

What you'll need:

- A dishwashing tub filled with water (a large bowl or bucket would also work)

- A bar of soap

- A towel to dry feet, as well as two or three towels to put under the tub of water.

- Read John 13 out loud, and ask the following questions:

    - Why was foot washing so important in Jesus' culture?
    - What was the social status of the person doing the foot washing?
    - What was Jesus teaching his disciples?
    - How did the disciples respond when Jesus began washing their feet? Explain your answer.
    - How might people today respond to having their feet washed? Why?

After discussing these questions, explain that you would like to serve some (or all) of the people in the room by washing their feet. Remind students that this is a way to honor them and show your appreciation for them.

After finishing, spend some time in prayer.

WHO IS JESUS?

Jesus is God

The high priest said to him, "I charge you under oath by the living God: Tell us if you are the Christ, the Son of God." "Yes, it is as you say," Jesus replied. (Matthew 26:63-64)

Jesus became a person

The Word [Jesus] became flesh and made his dwelling among us. (John 1:14)

Jesus taught with authority

They were amazed at his teaching, for he taught as one who had real authority—quite unlike the teachers of religious law. (Mark 1:22)

Jesus healed the sick

Jesus went throughout Galilee, teaching in their synagogues, preaching the good news of the kingdom, and healing every disease and sickness among the people. (Matthew 4:23)

Jesus befriended outcasts

That night Matthew invited Jesus and his disciples to be his dinner guests, along with his fellow tax collectors and many other notorious sinners. The Pharisees were indignant. "Why does your teacher eat with such scum?" they asked his disciples. (Matthew 9:10-11)

Jesus got angry with religious oppressors

How terrible it will be for you teachers of religious law and you Pharisees. Hypocrites! You are like whitewashed tombs—beautiful on the outside but filled on the inside with dead people's bones and all sorts of impurity. (Matthew 23:27)

Jesus was persecuted

The chief priests and the whole Sanhedrin were looking for false evidence against Jesus so that they could put him to death. But they did not find any, though many false witnesses came forward. Finally two came forward. (Matthew 26:59-60)

Jesus was tempted in every way

… for he [Jesus] faced all of the same temptations we do… (Hebrews 4:15)

Jesus never sinned

… he [Jesus] did not sin. (Hebrews 4:15)

But you know that he [Jesus] appeared so that he might take away our sins. And in him is no sin. (1 John 3:5)

Jesus died, rose from the dead, and continues to live to this day

But Christ has indeed been raised from the dead… (1 Corinthians 15:20)

Jesus made it possible to have a relationship with God

For God so loved the world that he gave his one and only Son, that whoever believes in him shall not perish but have eternal life. For God did not send his Son into the world to condemn the world, but to save the world through him. (John 3:16-17)

Jesus can sympathize with our struggles

This High Priest of ours understands our weaknesses… (Hebrews 4:15)

Jesus loves us

May you experience the love of Christ, though it is so great you will never fully understand it. (Ephesians 3:19)

Sound good? Looking for more?

Getting to know Jesus is the best thing you can do with your life. He WON'T let you down. He knows everything about you and LOVES you more than you can imagine!

A SUMMARY OF THE LIFE OF JESUS

The Incarnation

Fully divine and fully human, God sent his son, Jesus, to the earth to bring salvation into the world for everyone who believes. *Read John 1:4.*

John the Baptist

A relative to Jesus, John was sent "to make ready a people prepared for the Lord." He called Israel to repentance and baptized people in the Jordan River. *Read Luke 3:3.*

The baptism and temptation of Jesus

After John baptized him, Jesus went into the desert for 40 days in preparation for his ministry. He faced Satan and resisted the temptation he offered by quoting Scripture. *Read Matthew 4:4.*

Jesus begins his ministry

The world's most influential person taught with authority, healed with compassion, and inspired with miracles. *Read Luke 4:15.*

Jesus' model of discipleship

Jesus called everyone to follow him—without reservation—and to love God and others. *Read Luke 9:23, 57-62.*

The opposition

The religious "upper class" opposed Jesus, seeking to discredit him in the eyes of the people. Jesus criticized their hypocrisy and love of recognition. *Read Matthew 23:25.*

The great "I Am"

Jesus claimed to be the bread of life; the light of the world; the good shepherd; and the way, the truth, and the life. Each of these titles reveals essential truth about who he is. *Read John 14:6.*

The great physician

His words brought conviction and comfort; his actions shouted to the world his true nature. Healing the sick, Jesus demonstrated his power and authority by helping people where they needed it most so they might accept the truth. *Read Matthew 14:14.*

The great forgiver

Humanity's deepest need is forgiveness and freedom from the guilt of the past—which separates us from God. Only God has the power to forgive, and Jesus further demonstrated his divinity by forgiving the guilty. *Read Matthew 9:6.*

The disciples

Jesus chose 12 ordinary men to change the world. They weren't rich, powerful, or influential. They had shady pasts, often made huge mistakes, and were filled with doubts. In spite of these things, Jesus used them to build his church. *Read Mark 3:14.*

The final night

On the night before his death, Jesus spent the time preparing his disciples, and he spent time alone. Obedient to the Father, Jesus was committed to go to the cross to pay the penalty for our sins. *Read Mark 14:32 ff.*

The Crucifixion

Jesus died a real death on the cross for the sins of the world. His ultimate sacrifice is something all believers should remember often. *Read John 19:30.*

The Resurrection

After dying on the cross, Jesus was raised from the dead by God's power. This miracle has never been disproved and validates everything Jesus taught. *Read 1 Corinthians 15:55.*

Want a more detailed chronology of Jesus' life and ministry on earth? Check out these two Web sites: http://www.bookofjesus.com/bojchron. htm and http://mb-soft.com/believe/txh/gospgosp.htm

SMALL GROUP ROSTER

NAME	E-MAIL	PHONE	ADDRESS / CITY / ZIP CODE	SCHOOL/GRADE

HOW TO KEEP YOUR GROUP FROM BECOMING A CLIQUE

We all want to belong—God created us to be connected in community with one another. But the same drive that creates healthy community can also create negative community, often called a clique. A clique isn't just a group of friends—it's a group of friends uninterested in anyone outside their group. Cliques result in pain for those who are excluded.

If you read the second paragraph of the introduction (page 7), you see the words *spiritual community* used to describe your small group. If your small group becomes a clique, it's an unspiritual community. You have a clique when the biblical purpose of fellowship turns inward. That's ugly. It's the opposite of what God intended the body of Christ to be. Here's why:

- Cliques make your youth ministry look bad.

- Cliques make your small group appear immature.

- Cliques hurt the feelings of excluded people.

- Cliques contradict the value God places on each person.

- Few things are as unappealing as a youth ministry filled with cliques.

Many leaders avoid using their small groups as a way toward spiritual growth because they fear their groups will become cliques. But when they're healthy, small groups can improve your youth ministry's well-being, friendliness, and depth. The apostle Paul reminds us, "Be wise in the way you act toward outsiders; make the most of every opportunity" (Colossians 4:5).

Here are some ideas for being wise and preventing your small group from turning into a clique:

Be Aware

Learn to recognize when outsiders are uncomfortable with your group. It's easy to forget when you're an insider how bad it feels to be an outsider.

Reach Out

Once you're aware of someone feeling left out, make efforts to be friendly. Smile, shake hands, say hello, ask him or her to sit with you or your group, and ask simple yet personal questions. An outsider may come across as defensive, so be as accepting as possible.

Launch New Small Groups

Any small group with the attitude of "us four and no more" has become a clique. A time will come when your small group should launch into multiple small groups if it gets too big—because the bigger a small group gets, the less healthy it becomes. If your small group understands this, you can foster a culture of growth and fellowship.

For Students Only

Small group members expect adult leaders to confront them for acting like a clique. But instead of waiting for an adult to make the move, shock everyone by stepping up and challenging what you know is destructive. Take a risk. Be a spokesperson for your youth ministry and your student peers by leading the way. Be part of a small group that isn't cliquey and don't be afraid to challenge those who are.

SPIRITUAL HEALTH ASSESSMENT

Evaluating your spiritual journey is important—that's why we've encouraged you to take a brief survey at the end of each session. The following few pages are simply longer versions of the short evaluation tool that is at the end of each session.

Your spiritual journey will take you to low spots as well as high places. Spiritual growth is not a smooth incline—a loopy roller coaster is more like it. When you regularly consider your life, you'll develop an awareness of God's Spirit working in you. Evaluate. Think. Learn. Grow.

The assessment in this section is a tool, not a test. The purpose of this tool is to help you evaluate where you are in your faith journey. No one is perfect, so don't worry about your score. It won't be published in your church bulletin. Be honest so you have an accurate idea of how you're doing.

When you finish, celebrate the areas where you're relatively healthy and think about how you can use your strengths to help others on their spiritual journeys. Then think of ways your group members can help one another to improve weak areas through support and example.

FELLOWSHIP: CONNECTING YOUR HEART TO OTHERS

1. I meet consistently with a small group of Christians.

1	2	3	4	5
POOR				OUTSTANDING

2. I'm connected to other Christians who hold me accountable.

1	2	3	4	5
POOR				OUTSTANDING

3. I can talk with my small group leader when I need help, advice, or support.

1	2	3	4	5
POOR				OUTSTANDING

4. My Christian friends are a significant source of strength and stability in my life.

1	2	3	4	5
POOR				OUTSTANDING

5. I regularly pray for others in my small group outside of our meetings.

1	2	3	4	5
POOR				OUTSTANDING

6. I have resolved all conflicts with other people—both Christians and non-Christians.

1	2	3	4	5
POOR				OUTSTANDING

7. I've done all I possibly can to be a good son or daughter and brother or sister.

1	2	3	4	5
POOR				OUTSTANDING

TOTAL:_____

Take time to answer the following questions to further evaluate your spiritual health. You can do this after your small group meets if you don't have time during the meeting. If you need help with this, schedule a time with your small group leader to talk about your spiritual health.

8. List the three most significant relationships you have right now. Why are these people important to you?

9. How would you describe the benefit from being in fellowship with other Christians?

10. Do you have an accountability partner? If so, what have you been doing to hold each other accountable? If not, how can you get one?

DISCIPLESHIP: GROWING TO BE LIKE JESUS

11. I have regular times of conversation with God.

1	2	3	4	5
POOR				OUTSTANDING

12. I'm closer to God this month than I was last month.

1	2	3	4	5
POOR				OUTSTANDING

13. I'm making better decisions this month compared to last month.

1	2	3	4	5
POOR				OUTSTANDING

14. I regularly attend church services and grow spiritually as a result.

1	2	3	4	5
POOR				OUTSTANDING

15. I consistently honor God with my finances through giving.

1	2	3	4	5
POOR				OUTSTANDING

16. I regularly study the Bible on my own.

1	2	3	4	5
POOR				OUTSTANDING

17. I regularly memorize Bible verses or passages.

1	2	3	4	5
POOR				OUTSTANDING

TOTAL:_____

Take time to answer the following questions to further evaluate your spiritual health. You can do this after your small group meets if you don't have time during the meeting. If you need help with this, schedule a time with your small group leader to talk about your spiritual health.

18. What books or chapters from the Bible have you read during the last month?

19. What has God been teaching you lately from Scripture?

20. What was the last verse you memorized? When did you memorize it? Describe the last time a memorized Bible verse helped you.

MINISTRY: SERVING OTHERS IN LOVE

21. I am currently serving in some ministry capacity.

1	2	3	4	5
POOR				OUTSTANDING

22. I'm effectively ministering where I'm serving.

1	2	3	4	5
POOR				OUTSTANDING

23. Generally I have a humble attitude when I serve others.

1	2	3	4	5
POOR				OUTSTANDING

24. I understand God has created me as a unique individual, and he has a special plan for my life.

1	2	3	4	5
POOR				OUTSTANDING

25. When I help others, I typically don't look for anything in return.

1	2	3	4	5
POOR				OUTSTANDING

26. My family and friends consider me generally unselfish.

1	2	3	4	5
POOR				OUTSTANDING

27. I'm usually sensitive to others' hurts and respond in a caring way.

1	2	3	4	5
POOR				OUTSTANDING

TOTAL:_____

Take time to answer the following questions to further evaluate your spiritual health. You can do this after your small group meets if you don't have time during the meeting. If you need help with this, schedule a time with your small group leader to talk about your spiritual health.

28. If you're currently serving in a ministry, why are you serving? If not, what's kept you from getting involved?

29. What spiritual lessons have you learned while serving?

30. What frustrations have you experienced as a result of serving?

EVANGELISM: SHARING YOUR STORY AND GOD'S STORY

31. I regularly pray for my non-Christian friends.

1	2	3	4	5
POOR				OUTSTANDING

32. I invite my non-Christian friends to church.

1	2	3	4	5
POOR				OUTSTANDING

33. I talk about my faith with others.

1	2	3	4	5
POOR				OUTSTANDING

34. I pray for opportunities to share what Jesus has done in my life.

1	2	3	4	5
POOR				OUTSTANDING

35. People know I'm a Christian because of what I do, not just because of what I say.

1	2	3	4	5
POOR				OUTSTANDING

36. I feel strong compassion for non-Christians.

1	2	3	4	5
POOR				OUTSTANDING

37. I have written my testimony and am ready to share it.

1	2	3	4	5
POOR				OUTSTANDING

TOTAL:_____

Take time to answer the following questions to further evaluate your spiritual health. You can do this after your small group meets if you don't have time during the meeting. If you need help with this, schedule a time with your small group leader to talk about your spiritual health.

38. Describe any significant spiritual conversations you've had with non-Christians during the last month.

39. Have non-Christians ever challenged your faith? If yes, describe how.

40. Describe some difficulties you've faced when sharing your faith.

41. What successes have you experienced recently in personal evangelism? (Success isn't limited to bringing people to salvation directly. Helping someone take a step closer at any point on his or her spiritual journey is success.)

WORSHIP: SURRENDERING YOUR LIFE TO HONOR GOD

42. I consistently participate in Sunday and midweek worship experiences at church.

1	2	3	4	5
POOR				OUTSTANDING

43. My heart breaks over the things that break God's heart.

1	2	3	4	5
POOR				OUTSTANDING

44. I regularly give thanks to God.

1	2	3	4	5
POOR				OUTSTANDING

45. I'm living a life that, overall, honors God.

1	2	3	4	5
POOR				OUTSTANDING

46. I have an attitude of wonder and awe toward God.

1	2	3	4	5
POOR				OUTSTANDING

47. I often use the free access I have into God's presence.

1	2	3	4	5
POOR				OUTSTANDING

TOTAL:_____

Take time to answer the following questions to further evaluate your spiritual health. You can do this after your small group meets if you don't have time during the meeting. If you need help with this, schedule a time with your small group leader to talk about your spiritual health.

48. Make a list of your top five priorities. You can get a good idea of your priorities by evaluating how you spend your time. Be realistic and honest. Are your priorities are in the right order? Do you need to get rid of some or add new priorities? (As a student you may have some limitations. This isn't ammo for dropping out of school or disobeying parents!)

49. List 10 things you're thankful for.

50. What influences, directs, guides, or controls you the most?

DAILY BIBLE READINGS

As you meet with your small group for Bible study, prayer, and encouragement, you'll grow spiritually. But no matter how wonderful your small group experience, you need to learn to grow spiritually on your own, too. God has given you an incredible tool to help—his love letter, the Bible. The Bible reveals God's love for you and gives directions for living life to the fullest.

To help you with this, we've included a fairly easy way to read through one of the Gospels. Instead of feeling like you need to sit down and read the entire book at once, we've broken down the reading into bite-size chunks. Check off the passages as you read them. Don't feel guilty if you miss a daily reading. Simply do your best to develop the habit of being in God's Word daily.

A 30-Day Journey through the Gospel of Mark

Imagine sitting at the feet of Jesus himself: the Teacher who knows how to live life well, the Savior who died for you, the Lord who commands the universe. Like his first disciples, you can follow him around, watch what he does, listen to what he says, and pattern your life after his.

Day 1	Mark 1:1-20
Day 2	Mark 1:21-45
Day 3	Mark 2:1-12
Day 4	Mark 2:13-28
Day 5	Mark 3:1-19
Day 6	Mark 3:20-35
Day 7	Mark 4:1-20
Day 8	Mark 4:21-41
Day 9	Mark 5:1-20
Day 10	Mark 5:21-43
Day 11	Mark 6:1-29

HOW TO STUDY THE BIBLE ON YOUR OWN

The Bible is the foundation for all the books in the EXPERIENCING CHRIST TOGETHER series. Every lesson contains a Bible passage for your small group to study and apply. To maximize the impact of your small group experience, it's helpful if each participant spends time reading and studying the Bible during the week. When you read the Bible for yourself, you can have discussions based on what you know the Bible says instead of what another member has heard second- or third-hand about the Bible.

Growing Christians learn to study the Bible so they can grow spiritually on their own. Here are some principles about studying the Bible to help you give God's Word a central place in your life.

Choose a Time and Place

Since we are easily distracted, pick a time when you're at your best. If you're a morning person, then study the Bible in the morning. Find a place away from phones, computers, and TVs so you are less likely to be interrupted.

Begin with Prayer

Acknowledge God's presence with you. Thank him for his gifts, confess your sins, and ask for his guidance and understanding as you study his love letter to you.

Start with Excitement

We often take God's Word for granted and forget what an incredible gift we have. God wasn't forced to reach out to us, but he did. He's made it possible for us to know him, understand his directions, and be encouraged—all through his Word, the Bible. Remind yourself how amazing it is that God wants you to know him.

Read the Passage

After choosing a passage, read it several times. You might want to read it slowly, pausing after each sentence. If possible, read it out loud. (Remember that before the Bible was written on paper, it was spoken verbally from generation to generation.)

Keep a Journal

Respond to God's Word by writing down how you're challenged, truths to remember, thanksgiving and praise, sins to confess, commands to obey, or any other thoughts you have.

Dig Deep

When you read the Bible, look deeper than the plain meaning of the words. Here are a few ideas about what to look for:

- *Truth about God's character.* What do the verses reveal about God's character?

- *Truth about your life and our world.* You don't have to figure out life on your own. Life can be difficult, but when you know how the world works, you can make good decisions guided by wisdom from God.

- *Truth about the world's past.* The Bible reveals God's intervention in our mistakes and triumphs throughout history. The choices we read about—good and bad—serve as examples to challenge us to greater faith and obedience. (See Hebrews 11:1-12:1.)

- *Truth about our actions.* God will never leave you stranded. Although he allows us all to go through hard times, he is always with us. Our actions have consequences and rewards. Just like he does in Bible stories, God can use all of the consequences and rewards caused by our actions to help others.

As you read, ask these four questions to help you learn from the Bible:

- What do these verses teach me about who God is, how he acts, and how people respond?

- What does this passage teach about the nature of the world?

- What wisdom can I learn from what I read?

- How should I change my life because of what I learned from these verses?

Ask Questions

You may be tempted to skip over parts you don't understand, but don't give up too easily. Understanding the Bible can be hard work. If you come across a word you don't know, look it up in a regular dictionary or a Bible dictionary. If you come across a verse that seems to contradict another verse, see whether your Bible has any notes to explain it. Write down your questions and ask someone who has more knowledge about the Bible than you. Buy or borrow a study Bible or check the Internet. Try www.gotquestions.org or www.carm.org for answers to your questions.

Apply the Truth to Your Life

The Bible should make a difference in your life. It contains the help you need to live the life God intended. Knowledge of the Bible without personal obedience is worthless and causes hypocrisy and pride. Take time to consider the condition of your thinking, attitudes, and actions, and wonder about how God is working in you. Think about your life situation and how you can serve others better.

More Helpful Ideas

- Decide that the time you have set aside for Bible reading and study is nonnegotiable. Don't let other activities squeeze Bible study time out of your schedule.

- Avoid the extremes of being ritualistic (reading a chapter just to mark it off a list) and being lazy (giving up).

- Begin with realistic goals and boundaries for your study time. If five to seven minutes a day proves a challenge at the beginning, make it a goal to start smaller and increase your time slowly. Don't set yourself up to fail.

- Be open to the leading and teaching of God's Spirit.

- Love God like he's the best friend you'll ever have—which is the truth!

MEMORY VERSES

The word *memory* may cause some of you to groan. In school, you have to memorize dates, places, times, and outcomes. Now you have to memorize the Bible?

No, not the entire Bible! Start small with some key verses. Trust us, this is important. Here's why: Scripture memorization is a good habit for a growing Christian to develop because when God's Word is planted in your mind and heart, it has a way of influencing how you live. King David understood this: "I have hidden your word in my heart that I might not sin against you" (Psalm 119:11).

Challenge one another in your small group to memorize the six verses below—one for each time your small group meets. Hold each other accountable by asking about one another's progress. Write the verses on index cards and keep them available so you can learn and review them when you have a free moment (standing in line, before class starts, sitting at a red light, when you've finished a test and others are still working, waiting for your dad to get out of the bathroom—you get the picture). You'll be surprised at how many verses you can memorize as you work toward this goal and add verses to your list.

"FOR WHOEVER WANTS TO SAVE HIS LIFE WILL LOSE IT, BUT WHOEVER LOSES HIS LIFE FOR ME AND FOR THE GOSPEL WILL SAVE IT. WHAT GOOD IS IT FOR A MAN TO GAIN THE WHOLE WORLD, YET FORFEIT HIS SOUL?" —MARK 8:35-36

"SITTING DOWN, JESUS CALLED THE TWELVE AND SAID, 'IF ANYONE WANTS TO BE FIRST, HE MUST BE THE VERY LAST, AND THE SERVANT OF ALL.'" —MARK 9:35

"JESUS LOOKED AT THEM AND SAID, 'WITH MAN THIS IS IMPOSSIBLE, BUT NOT WITH GOD; ALL THINGS ARE POSSIBLE WITH GOD.'" —MARK 10:27

"FOR EVEN THE SON OF MAN DID NOT COME TO BE SERVED, BUT TO SERVE, AND TO GIVE HIS LIFE AS A RANSOM FOR MANY."
—MARK 10:45

"AND WHEN YOU STAND PRAYING, IF YOU HOLD ANYTHING AGAINST ANYONE, FORGIVE HIM, SO THAT YOUR FATHER IN HEAVEN MAY FORGIVE YOU YOUR SINS." —MARK 11:25

"'LOVE THE LORD YOUR GOD WITH ALL YOUR HEART AND WITH ALL YOUR SOUL AND WITH ALL YOUR MIND AND WITH ALL YOUR STRENGTH.' THE SECOND IS THIS: 'LOVE YOUR NEIGHBOR AS YOURSELF.' THERE IS NO COMMANDMENT GREATER THAN THESE." —MARK 12:30-31

JOURNALING: SNAPSHOTS OF YOUR HEART

In the simplest terms, journaling is reflection with pen in hand. A growing life needs time to reflect, so several times throughout this book you're asked to journal. In addition, you always have a journaling option at the end of each session. Through these writing opportunities, you're getting a taste of what it means to journal.

When you take time to write your thoughts in a journal, you'll experience many benefits. A journal is more than a diary—it's a series of snapshots of your heart. The goal of journaling is to slow down your life to capture some of the great, crazy, wonderful, chaotic, painful, encouraging, angering, confusing, joyful, and loving thoughts, feelings, and ideas in your life. Keeping a journal can become a powerful habit when you reflect on your life and how God is working in it.

Personal Insights

When confusion abounds in your life, disorderly thoughts and feelings often loom just out of range, slightly out of focus. Putting these thoughts and feelings on paper is like corralling and domesticating wild beasts. Once on paper, you can look at them, consider them, contemplate the reasons they were causing you pain, and learn from them.

Have you ever had trouble answering the question, "How do you feel?" Journaling compels you to become more specific with your generalized thoughts and feelings. This is not to suggest that a page full of words perfectly represents what's happening on the inside. That would be foolish. But journaling can move you closer to understanding more about yourself.

Reflection and Examination

With journaling, you can write about your feelings, your situations, how you responded to events. You can reflect and answer questions like these:

- Was that the right response?

- What were my other options?

- Did I lose control and act impulsively?

- If this happened again, should I do the same thing? Would I do the same thing?

- How can I be different as a result of this situation?

Spiritual Insights

One of the main goals of journaling is to gain new spiritual insights about God, yourself, and the world. When you take time to journal, you have the opportunity to pause and consider how God is working in your life and in the lives of those around you. Journaling helps you see the work he's accomplishing and remember it for the future.

What to Write About

There isn't one right way to journal, no set number of times per week, no rules for the length of each journal entry. Figure out what works best for you. Get started with these options:

Write a letter or prayer to God

Many Christians struggle with maintaining a consistent prayer life. Writing out your prayers can help strengthen it. Begin with this question: "What do I want to tell God right now?"

Write a letter or conversation to another person

Sometimes conversations with others can be difficult because we're not sure what we ought to say. Have you ever walked away from an interaction and 20 minutes later thought, *I should have said...*? Journaling conversations before they happen can help you think through the issues and approach your interactions with others in intentional ways. As a result, you can feel confident as you begin your conversations because you've taken time to consider the issues beforehand.

Process conflict and pain

You may find it helpful to write about your conflicts with others, especially those that take you by surprise. By journaling soon after conflict occurs, you can reflect and learn from it. You'll be better prepared for the next time you face a similar situation. Conflicts are generally difficult to navigate. Thinking through and writing about specific conflicts typically yields helpful personal insights.

When you're experiencing pain is also a good time to settle your thoughts and consider the nature of your feelings. The great thing about exploring your feelings is that you're only accountable to God. You don't have to worry about hurting anyone's feelings by what you write in your journal (if you keep it private).

Examine your motives

The Bible is clear regarding two heart truths. First, how you behave reflects who you are on the inside (Luke 6:45). Second, you can take the right action for the wrong reason (James 4:3).

The condition of your heart is vitally important. Molding your motives to God's desires is central to following Christ. The Pharisees did many of the right things, but for the wrong reasons. Reflect on the *real* reasons why you do what you do.

Anticipate your actions

Have you ever gone to bed thinking, *That was a mistake. I didn't intend that to happen!* Probably! No one is perfect. You can't predict all of the consequences of your actions. But reflecting on how your actions could affect others will guide you and help you relate better to others.

Reflect on God's work in your life

If you journal in the evening, you can answer this question: "What did God teach me today?"

If you journal in the morning, you can answer this question: "God, what were you trying to teach me yesterday that I missed?" When you reflect on yesterday's events, you may find a common theme that God may have been weaving into your life during the day—one you missed because you were busy. When you see God's hand in your life, even a day later, you know God loves you and is guiding you.

Record insights from Scripture

Journal about whatever you learn from the Bible. Rewrite a verse in your own words or figure out how a passage is structured. Try to uncover the key truths from the verses and see how the verses apply to your life. (Again, there is no right way to journal. The only wrong way is to not try it at all.)

JOURNAL PAGES

JOURNAL PAGES

JOURNAL PAGES

JOURNAL PAGES

JOURNAL PAGES

JOURNAL PAGES

PRAYING IN YOUR SMALL GROUP

As believers, we're called to support each other in prayer, and prayer should be a consistent part of a healthy small group.

One of prayer's purposes is aligning our hearts with God's. By doing this, we can more easily get in touch with what's at the center of God's heart. Prayer shouldn't be a how-well-did-I-do performance or a self-conscious, put-on-the-spot task to fear. Your small group may need time to get comfortable with praying out loud, too. That's okay.

When you do pray, silently or aloud, follow the practical, simple words of Jesus in Matthew 6:

Pray sincerely

"And when you pray, do not be like the hypocrites, for they love to pray standing in the synagogues and on the street corners to be seen by men. I tell you the truth, they have received their reward in full." (Matthew 6:5)

In the Old Testament, God's people were disciplined prayer warriors. They developed specific prayers to use for every special occasion or need. They had prayers for light and darkness, prayers for fire and rain, prayers for good news and bad. They even had prayers for travel, holidays, holy days, and Sabbath days.

Every day the faithful would stop to pray at 9 a.m., noon, and 3 p.m.—a sort of religious coffee break. Their ritual was impressive, to say the least, but being legalistic had its downside. The proud, self-righteous types would strategically plan their schedules to be in the middle of a crowd when it was time for prayer so everyone could hear them as they prayed loudly. You can see the problem. What was intended to promote spiritual passion became a drama to impress others.

God wants our prayers addressed to him alone. That seems obvious enough, yet how many of us pray wanting to impress our listeners rather than wanting to truly communicate with God? This is the problem if you're prideful like the Pharisees about the excellent quality of your prayers. But it can also be a problem if you're new to prayer and are concerned that you don't know how to "pray right." Don't concern yourself with what others think; just talk to God as if you were sitting in a chair next to him.

Pray simply

"And when you pray, do not keep on babbling like pagans, for they think they will be heard because of their many words. Do not be like them, for your Father knows what you need before you ask him." (Matthew 6:7-8)

God isn't looking to be dazzled with brilliantly crafted language. Nor is he impressed with lengthy monologues. It's freeing to know that he wants us to keep it simple.

Pray specifically

"This, then, is how you should pray: 'Our Father in heaven, hallowed be your name, your kingdom come, your will be done on earth as it is in heaven. Give us today our daily bread. Forgive us our debts, as we also have forgiven our debtors. And lead us not into temptation, but deliver us from the evil one." (Matthew 6:9-13)

What the church has come to call "The Lord's Prayer" is a model of the kind of brief but specific prayers we may offer anytime, anywhere. Look at some of the specific items mentioned:

- Adoration: "hallowed be your name"

- Provision: "your kingdom come...your will be done...give us today our daily bread"

- Forgiveness: "forgive us our debts"

- Protection: "lead us not into temptation"

PRAYER REQUEST GUIDELINES

Because prayer time is so vital, group members need some basic guidelines for sharing, handling, and praying for prayer requests. Without a commitment from each person to honor these simple suggestions, prayer time can become dominated by one person, an opportunity to gossip, or a never-ending story time. (There are appropriate times to tell personal stories, but this may not be the best time.)

Here are a few suggestions for each group to consider:

Write down prayer requests

Each small group member should write down every prayer request on the "Prayer Request" pages provided. When you commit to a small group, you're agreeing to be part of the spiritual community, and that includes praying for one another. By keeping track of prayer requests, you can see how God answers them. You'll be amazed at God's power and faithfulness.

As an alternative, one person can record the requests and e-mail them to the rest of the group. If your group chooses this option, safeguard confidentiality. Be sure personal information isn't compromised. Some people share e-mail accounts with parents or siblings. Develop a workable plan for this option.

Give everybody an opportunity to share

As a group, consider the amount of time remaining and the number of people who still want to share. You won't be able to share every thought or detail about a situation.

Obviously if someone experiences a crisis, you may need to focus exclusively on that group member by giving him or her extended time and focused prayer. (However, true crises are infrequent.)

The leader can limit the time by making a comment such as one of the following:

- We have time for everyone to share one praise or request.

- Simply share what to pray for. We can talk in more detail later.

- We're only going to pray for requests about the people in our group. How can we pray for you specifically?

- We've run out of time to share prayer requests. Take a moment to write down your prayer request and give it to me [or identify another person]. You'll get them by e-mail tomorrow.

Just as people are free to share, they're free to not share

The goal of a healthy small group should be to create an environment where participants feel comfortable sharing about their lives. Still, not everyone needs to share each week. Here's what I tell my small group:

As a small group we're here to support one another in prayer. This doesn't mean that everyone has to share something. In fact, don't assume you have to share at all. There's no need to make up prayer requests just to have something to say. If you have something you'd like the group to pray for, let us know. If not, that's fine, too.

No gossip allowed

Don't allow sharing prayer requests to become an excuse for gossip. If you're not part of the problem or solution, consider the information gossip. Share the request without the story behind it—that helps prevent gossip. Also speak in general terms without giving names or details ("I have a friend who's in trouble. God knows who it is. Pray for me that I can be a good friend.").

If a prayer request starts going astray, someone should kindly intercede, perhaps with a question such as, "How can we pray for you in this situation?"

Don't give advice or try to fix the problem

When people share their struggles and problems, a common response is to try to fix the problem by offering advice. At the right time, the group might provide input on a particular problem, but during prayer time, keep focused on praying for the need. Often God's best work in a person's life comes through times of struggle and pain.

Keep in touch

Make sure you exchange phone numbers and e-mail addresses before you leave the first meeting. That way you can contact someone who needs prayer or encouragement before the next time your group meets. You can write each person's contact information on the "Small Group Roster" (page 128).

PRAYER OPTIONS

There's no single, correct way to end all your sessions. In addition to the options provided in each session, here are some additional ideas.

During the Small Group Gathering

- One person closes in prayer for the entire group.

- Pray silently. Have one person close the silent prayer time after a while with "amen."

- The leader or another group member prays out loud for each person in the group.

- Everyone prays for one request or person. This can be done randomly during prayer or, as the request is shared, a willing person can announce, "I'll pray for that."

- Everyone who wants to pray takes a turn. Not everyone needs to pray out loud.

- Split the group into half and pray together in smaller groups.

- Pair up and pray for each other.

- On occasion, each person can share what he or she is thankful for before a prayer request, so prayer requests don't become negative from focusing only on problems. Prayer isn't just asking for stuff—it also includes praising God and being thankful for his generosity toward us.

- If you're having an animated discussion about a Bible passage or a life situation, don't feel like you must cut it short for prayer requests. Use it as an opportunity to add a little variety to the prayer time by praying some other day between sessions.

Outside the Group Time

You can use these options if you run out of time to pray during the meeting or in addition to prayer during the meeting.

- Send prayer requests to each other via e-mail.

- Pick prayer partners and phone each other during the week.

- Have each person in the small group choose a day to pray for everyone in the group. Perhaps you can work it out to have each day of the week covered. Let participants report back at each meeting for accountability.

- Have each person pray for just one other person in the group for the entire week. (Everyone prays for the person on the left or on the right or draw names.)

PRAYER REQUEST LOG

DATE	NAME	REQUEST	ANSWER

PRAYER REQUEST LOG

DATE | NAME | REQUEST | ANSWER

PRAYER REQUEST LOG

DATE	NAME	REQUEST	ANSWER

PRAYER REQUEST LOG

DATE	NAME	REQUEST	ANSWER

PRAYER REQUEST LOG

DATE	NAME	REQUEST	ANSWER

PRAYER REQUEST LOG

DATE   NAME   REQUEST   ANSWER

EXPERIENCING CHRIST TOGETHER FOR A YEAR

Your group will benefit the most if you work through the entire EXPE-RIENCING CHRIST TOGETHER series. The longer your group is together, the better your chances of maturing spiritually and integrating the biblical purposes into your life. Here's a plan to complete the series in one year.

Begin with a planning meeting and review the books in the series. They are:

Book 1—Beginning in Jesus: Six Sessions on the Life of Christ

Book 2—Connecting in Jesus: Six Sessions on Fellowship

Book 3—Growing in Jesus: Six Sessions on Discipleship

Book 4—Serving Like Jesus: Six Sessions on Ministry

Book 5—Sharing Jesus: Six Sessions on Evangelism

Book 6—Surrendering to Jesus: Six Sessions on Worship

We recommend you begin with *Book 1—Beginning in Jesus: Six Sessions on the Life of Christ,* because it contains an introduction to six qualities of Jesus. After that, you can use the books in any order that works for your particular ministry.

As you look at your youth ministry calendar, you may want to tailor the order in which you study the books to complement events your youth group will experience. For example, if you plan to have an evangelism outreach, study *Book 5—Sharing Jesus: Six Sessions on Evangelism* first to build momentum. Or study *Book 4—Serving Like Jesus: Six Sessions on Ministry* in late winter to prepare for the spring break missions trip.

Use your imagination and celebrate the completion of each book. Have a worship service, an outreach party, a service project, a fun night out, a meet-the-family dinner, or whatever else you can dream up.

Number of Weeks	Meeting Topic
1	Planning meeting—a casual gathering to get acquainted, discuss expectations, and refine the covenant (page 18).
6	Beginning in Jesus: Six Sessions on the Life of Christ
1	Celebration
6	Connecting in Jesus: Six Sessions on Fellowship
1	Celebration
6	Growing in Jesus: Six Sessions on Discipleship
1	Celebration
6	Serving Like Jesus: Six Sessions on Ministry
1	Celebration
6	Sharing Jesus: Six Sessions on Evangelism
1	Celebration
6	Surrendering to Jesus: Six Sessions on Worship
1	Celebration
2	Christmas Break
1	Easter Break
6	Summer Break

ABOUT THE AUTHORS

A youth ministry veteran of 25 years, **Doug Fields** has authored or co-authored more than 40 books, including *Purpose-Driven® Youth Ministry* and *Your First Two Years in Youth Ministry*. With an M.Div. from Fuller Theological Seminary, Doug is a teaching pastor and pastor to students at Saddleback Church in Southern California and president of Simply Youth Ministry. He and his wife, Cathy, have three children.

Brett Eastman has served as the leader of small groups for both Willow Creek Community Church and Saddleback Church. Brett is now the founder and CEO of LIFETOGETHER, a ministry whose mission is to "transform lives through community." Brett earned his masters of divinity degree from Talbot School of Theology and lives in Southern California.